20 Great BWCA Trips

Exploring the Boundary Waters Canoe Area

Preface

"When one finally arrives at the point where schedules are forgotten, and becomes immersed in ancient rhythms, one begins to live."

Sigurd Olson

Are you frequently stressed out by all the demands and activities of modern life? Does driving through rush hour traffic every morning leave you stressed out even before you get to work? Do you then spend eight, ten, or even more hours at tasks and meetings that bring little joy and often seem pointless? Do you also wish you could escape from all the communication "conveniences" of contemporary life, like the cell phone that never leaves you out of touch with the rest of humanity, or the email inbox that fills up faster than you can empty it? Wouldn't it also be nice to escape to some beautiful, natural place?

Or maybe you are a person who likes to get out in the world, to try new things, to test yourself against new challenges, to discover what is around the next bend or over the next hill? You probably also enjoy breathing pure, unpolluted air, feeling the wind blowing through your hair and the sun shining on your face.

We know of a place where you escape all the stresses of the modern world and enjoy the peace, quiet and joy of nature—all without spending much money. That place is the Boundary Waters Canoe Area (BWCA), located in the arrow-head region of northeastern Minnesota. There, cell phone service is spotty to nonexistent, there is no wireless internet, no email, and, in the BWCA, no roads and no cars. Furthermore, in most of the BWCA, there are no outboard motors or low-flying airplanes. If you choose, you can spend days, even weeks without communicating with another human being.

A vast and beautiful northern wilderness, the BWCA is filled with thousands of lakes, streams and rivers, millions of trees, pure, unpolluted air, and an almost endless sense of peace and quiet. Here you can walk forest footpaths originally blazed by Native Americans centuries ago, canoe thousands of beautiful lakes and streams, sleep under the stars, and follow the historic trail that the voyageurs used for about one hundred years on their annual trading trips.

With a little luck, you might see bald eagles soaring on the breeze, a cow moose and her calf wading in shallow waters near a wooded shore, and if you're really lucky, you may hear the eerie howling of a pack of wolves as they gather together in the early evening. No matter what, you're almost guaranteed to hear a variety of loon calls, and in the evening, after you've enjoyed a freshly caught walleye fillet cooked over an open campfire, you can watch the sun set and the mirror-like reflection of the sun's rays on the surface of a calm lake. After the sun has set, there is nothing better and more relaxing than sitting beside a campfire, listing to the crackling of the logs and watching the flames dance amid a bed of red and orange coals.

What a way to live—in beauty, on your own, doing whatever you want, whenever you want. Like Thoreau at his small cabin on Walden Pond, you can experience life at a primordial level, dependent solely on yourself and any traveling companions along with you. As the distinguished journalist Eric Sevareid once said, "There is cleanness, a breath and sweep and strength in the north, a purifying realization that one is living close to the fundamental elements of life. Yes, the north has a spell."

We have been going to the BWCA for thirty years and have never had the same trip twice. Every trip is a new adventure, where we discover new mysteries and return with fresh memories to take with us. Every trip has enriched our lives, and we plan to keep going back until the rigors of old age finally make this area exist only in our memories and the tales we tell our children and grandchildren.

Table of Contents

Preface 4

Introduction 8

Overview Map 10

Visiting the Boundary Waters 12

What You Should Know Before Leaving 13

BWCA Rules and Regulations 16

Equipment You Will Need 18

Food and Water 26

Some Packing Tips 28

Paddling 30

Camping 32

Camping and Canoeing with Younger Children 34

Fishing the BWCA 36

Suggested Equipment Checklist 40

How to Use this Book 43

West Area Trips 44

    Little Indian Sioux River (North) 46

    Mudro Lake 52

    Fall Lake 58

Wood Lake 64

Snowbank Lake 70

Lake One 76

Hegman Lake 82

Central Area Trips 88

Isabella Lake 90

Hog Creek 96

Kawishiwi Lake 102

Sawbill Lake 108

Baker Lake 114

Homer Lake 120

Brule Lake 126

East Area Trips 132

Missing Link Lake 134

Sea Gull Lake 140

Duncan Lake 146

Clearwater Lake 152

East Bearskin Lake 158

John Lake 164

About the Authors 170

Introduction

The Boundary Waters Canoe Area in northeastern Minnesota is a national treasure. It was listed as one of the *1,000 Places to See Before You Die* by Patricia Schultz, and has been featured in countless articles and books, including an issue of *National Geographic Traveler* magazine entitled "50 Places of a Lifetime." More importantly, the BWCA continues to draw thousands of visitors each year, all to a place with no cell phone reception, where there are no stores, and most, if not all, of modern conveniences are absent.

The BWCA has many beautiful, unique entry points, and contrary to popular belief, many are readily accessible. This book highlights twenty trips that provide newcomers and experts alike with easy access to the Boundary Waters Canoe Area.

So if you thought going to the BWCA required a long, rugged trip of a week or more and a marathon of portaging, think again. In this book, you can select from twenty short, manageable and memorable trips; these trips highlight the wonders of the vast wilderness, occur throughout the entire BWCA (giving you a sense of the scope and diversity of the area), yet aren't too mentally or physically taxing. In addition, we chose trips that we think will make you a BWCA fan for life. We hope that our trips will give you the confidence to return year after year and perhaps even tackle a longer trip.

With that said, we are assuming you have some camping and canoeing experience. If you've never camped or canoed, you should practice before entering the BWCA. If you are a beginning canoeist, it's probably best to travel with someone experienced in canoe travel. Beginners should also have some experience navigating with a map and compass. A handheld GPS unit can be of some assistance, but you'll still need a good map, as GPS systems don't indicate campsites and portages.

To stay up-to-date, we recently revisited each of these areas, and in our discussions of each trip, we do our best to pass on our knowledge about the BWCA and especially what we've learned from our own trips.

—Van Jordahl and Gerald Strom

Overview Map

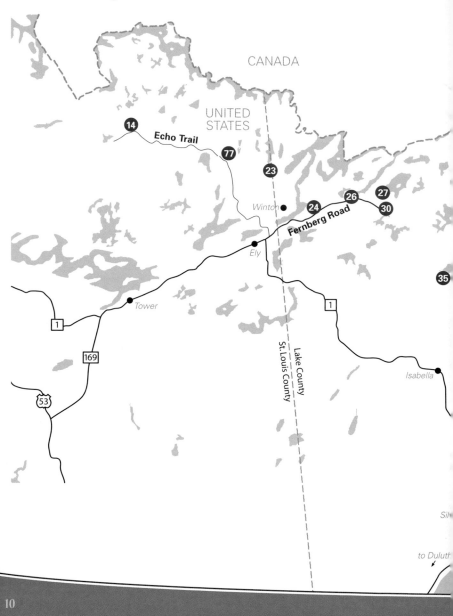

Note: There are many entry points to the BWCA. Each trip in this book begins at a separate entry point, and only those points are shown on this map.

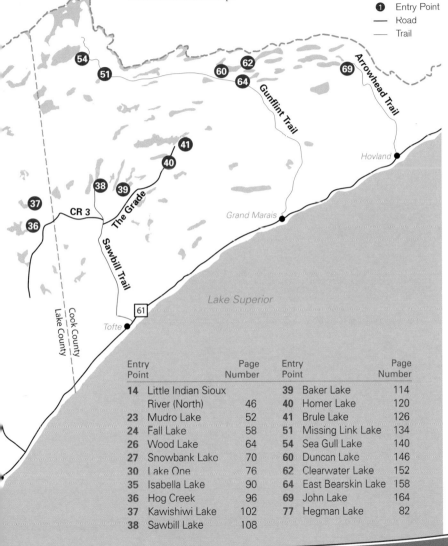

● Entry Point
— Road
— Trail

Entry Point		Page Number	Entry Point		Page Number
14	Little Indian Sioux River (North)	46	39	Baker Lake	114
23	Mudro Lake	52	40	Homer Lake	120
24	Fall Lake	58	41	Brule Lake	126
26	Wood Lake	64	51	Missing Link Lake	134
27	Snowbank Lake	70	54	Sea Gull Lake	140
30	Lake One	76	60	Duncan Lake	146
35	Isabella Lake	90	62	Clearwater Lake	152
36	Hog Creek	96	64	East Bearskin Lake	158
37	Kawishiwi Lake	102	69	John Lake	164
38	Sawbill Lake	108	77	Hegman Lake	82

Visiting the Boundary Waters

This book was written to help first-time visitors and experienced paddlers alike have a great experience in the BWCA. We have chosen trips that are relatively easy and feature a limited amount of paddling, yet trips that provide a genuine BWCA experience.

All of our trips are based upon the idea of base camping. This means that you enter and set up your base camp, and then day-trip around the area from that camp. This allows you to explore the lake you're camping on, and you can portage to other nearby lakes. The great advantage of this is that you do not have to pack up all your equipment each morning, move to another site, and then set up your camp all over again. You set up camp once and day-trip from there, and you don't need to paddle and portage all day, expending thousands of calories. Instead, you can plan a trip that involves just as much paddling and portaging as you're comfortable with; in fact, a number of the trips in this book involve no portaging at all.

All our trips are designed to last about three or four days. From our own experience, we have found that this is about the right amount of time to spend in the BWCA for many people. When you come out after three or four days, you'll have had a great BWCA experience but you'll be glad to return to "civilization."

Finally, these trips are designed so that you exit at the same point you first entered the BWCA. This makes it less likely you'll get lost, and it has another great advantage: when you exit the BWCA, your car or SUV is waiting, making it simple to load up and be on your way.

What You Should Know Before Leaving

The BWCA is a vast wilderness largely untouched by humans. When you are in the BWCA, you will be completely on your own and will have only what you initially brought along. There are no stores, no electricity, no roads, and no cell phone coverage or internet access. You, and the other members of your party, will exist as if you are on an isolated island, cut off by woods and water from the rest of modern civilization. Everyone in your party should be in good physical condition, and it helps if you have some previous camping experience.

Your Health

The most important thing to consider before entering the BWCA is your physical condition. You don't need to be a fit athlete but you should be in good health. You must be able to paddle a canoe, sometimes against both winds and waves. If you're planning on portaging to a lake, you must be able to portage (carry) your equipment over trails that are usually not flat and often rocky. Before you set off on a BWCA trip, consider seriously whether or not you have the physical strength and stamina required. The BWCA is not accessible for many with physical handicaps.

Permits

Another important factor to consider is that the BWCA operates on a permit system. If you plan an overnight stay in the BWCA between May 1st and September 30th, you need an entry permit (see page 15 for out-of-season permits), and there is a limit on how many permits are issued for each entry point each day. To acquire a permit, you have two basic choices.

The best strategy is to apply for a permit in advance. If you apply online at www.recreation.gov between December 1st and January 15th, your application will be included in a lottery held January 15th. If you apply after January 15th, you can do so in three ways, (1) online at www.recreation.gov, (2) by calling the BWCAW Reservation Center at (877) 550-6777, or (3) by mailing your application to the BWCAW Reservation Center, PO Box 462, Ballston Spa, NY 12020.

We've found that it's best to use the website www.recreation.gov as it allows you to check which entry points have permits available on the days you want to enter. You can then make a reservation for one of the open dates.

If you don't get a permit in advance, you can also drive to the area and attempt to get a permit, either from one of the Forest Service offices in Ely or Grand Marais, or from a designated permit issuer. A list of permit issuers can be found online at www.bwca.cc/tripplanning/permitissuers.htm.

However, if you choose this option, you are taking a big gamble because each entry point has a daily entry quota. If the entry point you want has its quota filled for the day you want to enter, you will have to try for a different entry point or visit on a different day. You should also be aware that most people visit the BWCA in July and August, so plan accordingly. If you can avoid those times your choices will be better.

Whichever of these methods you use, your group will be charged several fees. There is a nonrefundable application fee, and there are fees for each adult and for each child under 18 and senior over 65. See www.recreation.gov for current prices. After you pay your fees, you and your group can stay in the BWCA for as long as you want, though you can only stay at each campsite for a maximum of 14 days. Also, you must apply for a specific entry point and a specific day, but you can specify alternative acceptable entry points and days.

Once you are issued a permit, the person designated as the team leader or a specified alternate must pick up the permit at a designated permit issuing station. You can pick it up the day before you plan to enter, or on the day of entry. The team leader or alternate must be with your party the entire time you are in the BWCA.

You should also be aware that there are three other kinds of permits for entering the BWCA. These are easy to get and cost nothing.

Day Permits: If you enter the BWCA and aren't staying overnight (and you're not using a motor of any kind) there is no charge for a permit, and you can issue it to yourself. Just drive to the entry point you want, fill out the permit form kept in a box there, and deposit the form back in the box. There are no quotas for these permits.

Out-of-Season Permits: If you enter for an overnight stay between October 1st and April 30th, the same permit exists. But if you plan to stay overnight, you must deposit the form along with $16 for every adult and $8 for every child under the age of 18 and every senior over the age of 65. Like day permits, there are no quotas on out-of-season permits.

Motor Permits: Motors of 25 horsepower and under are allowed on a few lakes in the BWCA. As we are only concerned with canoe trips in this book, we forgo detailing the complicated process of getting such a permit.

BWCA Rules and Regulations

In addition to an entry permit, there are a number of other rules and regulations you need to know about and observe. Two of these are not official rules but should be observed by everyone. One of these is the basic axiom: Leave No Trace. This means that the next people who use your campsite should see no evidence that you were ever there.

A second unofficial rule protects you in case you get lost or have an accident. Before leaving for your trip, let someone who is not going along know where you plan to go and where and when you plan to exit. When you exit, call them as soon as you can and let them know you are safely out. If you don't call within a reasonable time, your informant should contact the Forest Service authorities and give them information about what you were planning to do in the BWCA. This helps the authorities find you if you get lost, which is possible even with good maps or a GPS. As well as the two unofficial rules noted above, there are a number of official regulations governing BWCA travel that you need to be aware of.

No Motorized Boats Allowed: As the name indicates, the BWCA is a largely dedicated to canoeing, and the use of motorized boats is banned on almost all of the lakes in the BWCA. On some lakes the use of motors under 25 horsepower is allowed, though this requires a special permit. In addition, some lakes are divided into sections that allow motors and sections that only allow paddling, but as a general rule, motorboats aren't allowed in the BWCA.

Camping: In the BWCA, you can camp only in officially designated campsites. These are not reserved by your permit to enter. These all have primitive latrines and fire grates, and so are easy to identify. You can stay at any given campsite for a maximum of 14 consecutive days. Only nine people and four canoes are allowed in any one party and all must use the same campsite.

Banned Means of Transportation: Sailboats, pontoon boats, ATVs and sailboards are also prohibited. Finally, note that portage wheels are generally prohibited. They are allowed only on the Fall-Newton-Pipestone, Black Bay, Four Mile, and Prairie portages into Basswood Lake and on the Vermillion-Trout Lake portage.

Containers: Cans and glass bottles are not allowed so you need to repack their contents into zip-lock bags or plastic containers that you pack out with you when you leave. Fuel in metal containers for camp stoves is allowed, but containers also need to be packed out. Medicines, insect repellents, and personal toiletries are allowed as long as they are in plastic containers.

Waste: Always use the latrines at campsites to do your business and never use a lake or river as a toilet. Dogs are allowed in the BWCA, but their waste needs to be cleaned up and, if at a campsite, deposited in the latrines. If you're not at a campsite, such waste should be buried well back from any trail, lake or stream. Fish remains should also be buried at least 150 feet back from the campsite, trail or water. This is also a safety precaution as fish waste can attract bears.

Campfires: Only light fires in fire grates at campsites, and then only when there is no fire ban in effect in the area you are visiting. You can ask any outfitter in Ely or Grand Marais or check at the Forest Service office about the existence of fire bans. If campfires are allowed, use only deadwood you find lying on the ground and well away from your campsite or trail. This is an official rule, but it is also the only practical way to collect wood, as previous campers will already have used all of the good deadwood near the camp. You are not allowed to bring wood from outside the BWCA.

Metal Detectors and Historical Sites: Metal detectors are not allowed, and historical sites, archaeological sites, and rock paintings should not be disturbed in any way.

Equipment You Will Need

There are two factors to keep in mind in deciding what equipment to bring along with you on your trip. First, you will likely have to carry it over portages, so weight is an important factor. Second, it will have to stand up to use in a rugged wilderness, so get good quality equipment. We recommend that you bring high-quality lightweight equipment.

Canoes and Canoe Equipment

The single most important piece of equipment you will need for your BWCA trip is a canoe. If you already own one you are well on your way to a great adventure. However, if you don't own a canoe, you have two basic choices: you

Plastic Canoes

can buy one or rent one from an outfitter near the BWCA. If you have little experience canoeing and are not sure how you will enjoy it, we would suggest you rent instead of buying. In either case, there are a number of factors to consider when getting your canoe.

Size: By far the most popular canoes for use in the BWCA are 16- or 17-foot-long, two-person canoes. These canoes provide enough space to carry all the things that two or even three people will need on a BWCA trip.

Construction: Today, canoes are made from a variety of different materials, each of which has advantages and disadvantages.

Aluminum: For many years, the standard BWCA canoe was made of aluminum because aluminum is both strong and light. These canoes can withstand the rigors of the BWCA and are relatively easy to carry on a portage.

Plastic Composite: Recent years have seen many canoes made from a variety of different plastic composite materials. Many of these are as rugged as aluminum canoes, but they also tend to be heavier, making them hard to carry on portages. This disadvantage is offset by the fact that they generally cost much less to buy or rent.

Kevlar: Some of the lightest canoes you can get today are made from a material known as Kevlar. This makes them very popular for people who portage a lot. They also have a lower drag coefficient in the water, which makes them easier to paddle. Two downsides of these canoes are that they generally cost

Kevlar Canoe

more than either aluminum or composite canoes, and they are not nearly as rugged. You generally have to enter and exit them in shallow water because pulling them up on the rocks on shore can scratch and damage them. You must also be very careful to avoid damage from shallow rocks, especially in streams.

Canoe Licenses: If you rent a canoe, the outfitter will have purchased a license for it from the State of Minnesota. However, if you buy a canoe, you will also need to buy a license from the Minnesota Department of Natural Resources or your local courthouse. Canoes licensed outside of Minnesota are legal.

Canoe Transportation: As cars (and canoes) vary greatly in size and shape, ask your dealer, an outfitter, or a friend with experience in the BWCA how to secure your canoe to your car. We recommend purchasing a Yakima or Thule rack that fits your car (but these are expensive). A standard car rack usually works too, or can rent one from an outfitter

Other Canoe Equipment

Paddles: In addition to a canoe, you will need a paddle for each person. Be sure to bring one extra paddle, just in case something happens to one of the others. Matching the paddle length to the user is very important for ease of use and for a powerful stroke. When set on the floor, the top of the paddle should come up to the height of your nose.

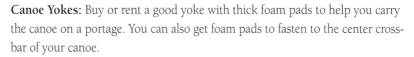

Canoe Yokes: Buy or rent a good yoke with thick foam pads to help you carry the canoe on a portage. You can also get foam pads to fasten to the center cross-bar of your canoe.

Life Vests: You need an approved life vest for each person in your canoe. Because canoes tip easily, each person should always wear their life vest when in the canoe. There should never be an exception to this rule.

Ropes: Whenever we are in the BWCA, we tie floating 20-foot nylon ropes to both the front and back of the canoe. Coil the front one toward the bottom of the canoe (but be careful that it doesn't entangle your feet) and keep the other rope toward the back of the canoe. The ropes, especially the one on the back, are for safety, giving you something to grab onto if your canoe overturns. Always stay with your canoe if you capsize, as it will float. The ropes are also good for attaching an anchor and pulling the canoe up on shore and securing it.

Gloves: Some paddlers develop blisters on their hands from paddling. One solution to this problem is a set of thin nylon gloves. Nylon works well, because it protects the skin from the paddle and dries out fast when it gets wet.

Navigation Equipment

Maps: The BWCA is the wilderness, and if you're not careful, it's possible to get lost. This is especially true on big lakes, lakes with complicated shorelines, or lakes with many islands (islands that many maps unfortunately do not show). To successfully navigate in the BWCA, you need detailed maps. Google maps will not work, although a detailed Google map of a given lake will show many of the islands that the standard maps do not include. In particular, your maps should show the precise locations of campsites, portages, and entry and exit points. Fortunately, three private companies issue appropriate maps. The three companies are: W. A. Fisher Company (www.fishermapsmn.com), McKenzie Maps (www.mckenziemaps.com) and Voyageur Maps (www.voyageurmaps.com.) You can also purchase these maps online at www.latitudemapstore.net, www.bwcamaps.com, and at the Piragis store in Ely (www.piragis.com).

Map Details: In order to provide the corresponding amount of detail for travel in the BWCA, each map covers only a small portion of the BWCA. This means that you need to find the map or maps that cover the areas you plan to travel in. Fortunately, all these maps are printed on waterproof paper. Even so, it's best to carry your maps in a large zip-lock bag. In order of detail, Voyageur maps are the least detailed and would likely be good for those who want to base-camp and take day trips. They are also very good at showing the roads you need to travel to get to your entry point. Fisher maps are somewhat more detailed, at 1.5 inches to a mile, and McKenzie maps, at 2 inches to a mile, are the most detailed. We strongly recommend that you get a McKenzie map if you are planning a trip on a complex lake, like Lake One, where there are many islands and peninsulas that can be confusing without a detailed map.

A Good Compass: Along with a good map, you will also need a good compass to help you successfully navigate. Of course, it is always wise to bring a spare.

GPS Navigation: You might also consider bringing a small, portable GPS navigation device along with your maps. Modern GPS units are very accurate, and some even allow you to download precise maps of lakes with contour depth lines included. (This can be very good for locating good fishing areas.) If you mark your entry point, GPS units can also help you get back to it without getting lost. The downside of some GPS units is that they have self-contained batteries that can only be charged with an electrical outlet or a car cigarette lighter. In this case, if your battery runs out, the unit is useless. The same is true if you drop and break your unit or it gets wet and no longer works. A GPS shouldn't be your only navigational aid; you need to have detailed maps and a good compass. If possible, bring a GPS unit with replaceable batteries, and bring extra batteries along. Always carry it in a padded and waterproof container. We used a small, handheld Garmin GPS unit to get the coordinate of each of the entry points given in this book.

Tents and Tarps

Tents: In the Boundary Waters you spend about the same amount of time in your tent as in your canoe. Fortunately, today tents appropriate for the BWCA are readily available at any reasonably sized sporting goods store at very affordable prices. From our experience, there are five basic criteria for a good BWCA tent.

Weight: It should be lightweight, so as not to overtax you when you have to carry it on a portage.

Size: It should be small in size, just big enough to sleep two persons while storing their clothes and other personal items.

Other Characteristics: Your tent should be waterproof; canvas or fabric tents can be problematic. It should be constructed so that each of the occupants can get out a door without having to crawl over the other person. Also, it should be easy to set up, and you should know how to set it up. Practice at home before you leave.

Tarps: Tarps can be useful when camping, as they can help keep the inside of your tent dry. Many campers put a tarp inside their tent to form an extra barrier against moisture.

Clothing

For a three- to five-day trip into the BWCA, we recommend that you bring one change of clothes along with the clothes you wear when entering the BWCA. You can take two changes if you prefer, but remember that this adds additional weight that you will have to carry on portages.

Type of Clothes to Bring Along: As to the type of clothing to bring, you will need a change or two of underpants and T-shirts, several pairs of socks, and two pairs of shoes, in case one pair gets wet. You might also want to bring along some boots or rubber shoes in case you end up on a muddy portage or rain soaks your camp. Some people prefer waterproof hiking boots.

Long Pants and Long-sleeved Shirts: For outer garments, we strongly recommend long-sleeved shirts and long pants. There are several reasons for this, even though it can get very hot in the BWCA in the summer. The first reason is the sun. Paddling on a lake is an activity that affords no shade and, without a long-sleeved shirt, you will need to wear sunscreen to avoid sunburn. (This is also why you should wear a wide-brimmed hat that protects your face and ears from the sun.) Mosquitoes and other biting insects are another reason to cover up. (Light-colored clothes are best, as mosquitoes are attracted to dark clothing.)

Weather is also a concern; in summer, two seasons actually exist in the BWCA: summer and fall. It can get cold, even in July and August, especially in the evening and at night. Short-sleeved shirts and short pants will not protect you against these chills.

On the other hand, if you have a nice breeze, are mostly in the shade, or have a high tolerance for the sun, feel free to bring some shorts and short-sleeved shirts along.

Be Prepared for Rain: It rains in the BWCA in the summer, so it's wise to bring a poncho or a rain suit that you can easily get into if a sudden storm arises.

Bathing and Swimming: Bring both a swimming suit and a pair of shoes designed for walking in water. The swimming suit allows you to take a cooling dip after a long day of paddling and, with a bar of biodegradable soap and shampoo, allows you to take a cleansing bath. We recommend the water shoes because BWCA lakes generally do not have nice sandy bottoms. Rather, the bottoms have a thin layer of mud and decaying vegetation on them and, in some places, some pretty sharp rocks.

Insect Repellent

We give special attention to insect repellent because of the prevalence of biting critters in the BWCA. You can expect to encounter mosquitoes, wood ticks, and black flies. A wide variety of repellents are available, and you will have to decide what will work for you. From our experience, the most effective of these repellents contain some DEET, but some people are allergic to DEET, and DEET should not be used on young children. If you don't like using chemical repellents, consider buying a hat with an insect screen that will keep the bugs off your face and neck. And you can prevent picking up most wood ticks by either avoiding grassy areas where ticks hang out or by tucking your pant bottoms into your socks. Even so, you should do a full body scan each evening to make sure you haven't picked up a wood tick.

Sunscreen

Remember to bring sunscreen along with you. Use sunscreen on all exposed skin, and remember that sunlight reflects off the water, so cover up whenever possible. Use sunscreen that is SPF 15 or higher, and use SPF 30 or higher on children.

First-Aid Kits

A first-aid kit is a must. You can assemble your own or purchase one, but your kit should be lightweight, waterproof, and include the essentials, including bandages, pain relievers, anti-itch creams (such as hydrocortisone), medicines for diarrhea/constipation and tweezers. See www.redcross.org for a full checklist. (Don't forget to bring along your personal prescriptions!)

Food and Water

Water Purification and Storage

When traveling to the BWCA, you can filter and/or treat lake water once you arrive in the BWCA. If you're traveling to a drop-in entry point where no portaging is required, bringing potable water along with you is easy, as weight isn't a concern. (All of the BWCA lakes that allow motors are drop-in lakes.) To bring water along, fill a large container or containers (at least five gallons) with water before you enter the lake. To store your water on your trip, bring along several large plastic, collapsible bottles (several gallons or larger) and some smaller plastic ones to carry with you in the canoe. Of course, be sure to bring enough water for your entire trip.

If you don't want to bring all of your water along, you have three options. You can bring along a water filter, treat your water with purification tablets, or you can boil your water. *Do not drink untreated lake, river or stream water*, as it can lead to an intestinal infection called giardiasis, more commonly known as "beaver fever." This will ruin your BWCA trip, or make you sick when the trip is over.

If you're filtering your water, hand pump water filters or gravity water filters work best, but filter quality and capability varies so make sure that the filter you purchase removes giardia. Purification tablets and boiling your water can also work, but tablets tend to leave an unpleasant taste, and boiling consumes more firewood than you may find. If you're planning to camp on a BWCA lake that allows motors, bring your water with you, as we know of no filter that removes petroleum or other chemical by-products.

Food

The availability of light, low cost freeze-dried and dehydrated foods has dramatically improved both the quality and variety of food you can bring along on your trip. You can buy this kind of food at many outdoor and camping stores for relatively high prices. Most freeze-dried food is cooked, spiced and ready to eat in a short time. On the other hand, you can get everything you need much more cheaply at your local supermarket. Check the packaging and select items that require small amounts of water and that have short cooking times. Keep in mind that while you are traveling and exploring in the BWCA you will consume more calories so we often use a two-portion meal as a single meal for one adult. Use your own judgment for your group, and don't underpack or you might end up very hungry toward the end of your trip. Also consider that weather may strand you for a day or two, and you may need some extra food.

Items to Add to the Grocery List

Just because you're in the wilderness doesn't mean you have to eat like it. Here are some tried-and-true meals we have to suggest.

Potatoes: Foil-wrapped, freeze-dried or dehydrated mashed potatoes are available from several companies and in many flavors. Get ones that have a preparation time of one to four minutes.

Pasta and Rice Dishes: Many such dishes are available, including fried rice and a wide variety of noodle dishes with sauce. Preparation time on a camp stove is usually around 7 minutes.

Meats and Fish: (no refrigeration until opened) Tuna and salmon in aluminum packages, smoked meats, sausages, and fully cooked bacon are all available.

Other Camp Foods: Some camp foods aren't meals in themselves, but are required to make some popular BWCA fare. Examples include powdered eggs, margarine, bread, tortillas, salt and pepper, peanut butter, cooking oil, pancake mix, fish breading, and the like.

Personal Food Items and Snacks: We recommend a fanny pack for each camper for carrying snacks and items such as nuts, trail mix, granola bars and candy bars. Always remember that fanny packs need to go into the regular food pack at night; this prevents run-ins with bears.

Some Packing Tips

When packing for your BWCA trip, it is helpful to separate your gear into two different categories. The first category consists of gear you will need on your trip to your campsite. This includes maps, a compass, water bottles, snacks, and a rain suit or poncho. These generally fit into a small backpack or fanny pack. What is important here is that you have easy access to them in the canoe.

The second category includes things you will not need until you reach your camp. This includes all your clothes, food, tents, sleeping bags and cooking equipment. For all this equipment, you need several good travel packs.

Travel Packs

In bringing along all your clothes and other gear, you will need to consider how you will transport it. The traditional way of carrying things in the BWCA is to use Duluth packs, manufactured in Duluth by the Duluth Tent and Awning Company. There are at least three reasons such packs have been favored for many years by experienced BWCA travelers. First, they are very strong and well constructed; secondly, they come in a large variety of shapes and sizes, and finally, most come with back straps, making them relatively easy to carry on a portage. You can get Duluth packs at their store in Duluth on online at www.duluthpack.com.

There are, however, two additional things to consider about Duluth packs. Since they are made out of a heavy-grade canvas, they tend to weigh more than other kinds of backpacks. Second, they are relatively expensive to purchase. Spending the extra money is well worth it if you plan to make many trips into the BWCA. But if you only plan on one or just a few such trips, the considerably cheaper but less rugged nylon backpacks sold by most large sporting goods stores should be considered. You might also consider the packs sold by the *Boundary Waters Journal* at www.boundarywatersjournal.com.

Packing

For two people, you should have three packs. The first should be a large group pack containing the pots and pans, cups and plates, silverware, a small cook-stove and fuel, a tent, a small axe and saw, insect repellent, fire starter, the sleeping bags, toilet paper, and whatever else you need for the whole group (see the checklist on page 40). The second pack is your food pack, containing all the food. (It's helpful to organize the food by breakfast, lunch and dinner.) The third pack contains both your clothes and personal items. For four people, add one extra clothes and personal items pack. This will greatly facilitate your ability to efficiently portage.

Double Bagging

It rains in the BWCA, and you need to keep your equipment dry. The best way to do this is to double bag all nonmetallic equipment in large, heavy-duty plastic garbage bags. Pack these large plastic garbage bags with as much as will fit into your backpack or other bag. Now tie the end closed with a twist tie. Then put the bag, twist-tie side in first, into another plastic garbage bag and put on another twist tie. Then slide the double-bagged package into your pack.

Paddling

With your permit and equipment in hand, you are ready to start your trip into the BWCA. Most of the routes we suggest are on small lakes and rivers and have short or moderate portages. On these trips, you'll travel on the water and over portages.

Most beginners in good health can paddle a loaded canoe an average of two to three miles per hour in good weather conditions. Of course, if the wind is at your back, your speed may improve, but if you are paddling into a moderate wind it may slow you down a bit.

If you are on a large lake route always check weather, waves and wind conditions. Stay on shore if you don't feel comfortable paddling in the conditions. If conditions change while you are paddling, head for the nearest shore or a protected area, and be prepared to wait it out. On large lakes, paddle close to shore so you can seek shelter. Get off the water if you hear thunder or see lightning.

When traveling on rivers or streams, you may encounter rapids. Do not run them; instead, we suggest beginners use all the designated portages. As the old canoe adage goes, "Nobody has ever drowned on a portage."

Portages are measured in rods, and canoe maps will list portage length by this measure. A rod is 16.5 feet, approximately one canoe length. Here are some ways to look at portage length:

¼ mile = 80 rods, ½ mile = 160 rods, 1 mile = 320 rods

Time spent on portages depends on the length of the portage, how rugged it is, or whether you single or double portage. Single portaging is simply carrying everything across the portage in one trip. We recommend that most beginners double portage. On a double portage each person carries one pack to the middle of the portage and sets it off to the side of the trail. They then return to the beginning of the portage for the remaining equipment and the canoe. Then continue to the end of the portage with your pack and the canoe, where you set the canoe off to the side and the pack off to the side. Finally, return to the middle of the portage to retrieve the original packs and return to the end of the portage. The portage is complete, and you are ready to load and return to the water. This method is easier than single portaging but takes at least twice as long. Your choice will depend on the size and weight of your packs and your physical condition. We currently double portage on almost all but the shortest and flattest portages.

Camping

A successful trip to the BWCA requires a good campsite, which are on a first-come first-serve basis and cannot be reserved. In the BWCA you must camp at designated campsites; these can be hard to spot from the water, and to find many of them, you often need a detailed map of the area.

Campsites can often be picked over quickly. Start your search for an open site relatively early in the day, no later than 2 or 3 p.m. The trips we suggest are easy, and you may have competition for available sites. If the only site on the lake is occupied, you will have to move on to the next available site, and that may require more paddling and portaging. This is why we stress that you take the first available site.

Selecting a Tent Site

Each tent site needs a flat area without protruding tree roots or rocks. Avoid depressions where water will gather if it rains. Don't camp too close to the fire grate, and keep in mind that underlying rock of the BWCA can be a problem for tent stakes. You may have to drive them at an odd angle to secure your tent. Metal tent stakes work better than plastic ones in the BWCA.

Canoe access: On most Canadian Shield lakes you should look for a flat landing on a rock shelf. Sandy sites are nice, but you will be tracking sand into your tents.

Firewood and Campfires: Dry wood may be scarce on well-used BWCA sites. You may have to go way back into the woods to find dead wood. You may also need to take your canoe along the lake to look for dry wood away from camp. Be aware that wood fires in a grate do not provide much heat for cooking. We suggest you bring a small camp stove (gas or propane) for most of your cooking.

Keeping Your Equipment and Clothes Dry: Store your clothes in a waterproof bag in your tent. We also suggest bringing a small tarp to use as a cover for your fishing gear, firewood, stove, and other equipment. Remember to tie it down and weight the end so it doesn't blow away.

Latrines: In BWCA campsites, the latrines are generally located away from the main campsite. Look for a path that leads back into the woods from your camp. If you're not near a latrine, bury your waste, and be sure to do so well away from any trail, lake or stream. Also, remember: never dispose of uneaten food in a latrine. It should be burned in your fire or buried well away from your camp.

Food Storage: Never take any food into your tents as this can cause bears to rip open your tent to get at it. Also, do not leave food or food scraps anywhere in your camp. We have camped for over thirty years, and although we have seen bears, we've never had a bear in our clean campsites. To prevent unwanted visits, always keep all your food in a waterproof bear pack; these are usually hung about 20 feet off the ground away from your camp. To hang a bear pack, take a small rock and tie or tape some fishing line to it. Then throw this over a tree branch at least 20 feet off the ground. Now tie a strong rope to the fishing line, and pull it over the branch. Tie one end of this rope to your food pack, and pull it to within 3 to 4 feet of the branch. Retrieve the end of the rope and tie the end in your hand to a tree. Only lower the pack to get the food you need for your current meal and then raise it again. In some areas of the BWCA (especially areas affected by the 1999 Blowdown), finding a good bear pack tree can be difficult. Fortunately, many outfitters now stock a bear barrel. As the name implies, this is a somewhat large, strong plastic barrel that can be sealed at each end so a bear cannot get at the food you packed inside. You can also use these barrels to keep food dry. If you use a bear barrel, line it with plastic garbage bags to minimize any food odor and always store it some distance from your main camp.

Camping and Canoeing with Younger Children

A family camping trip into the BWCA pro-vides an excellent way to teach kids about the wonders of the natural world and will help them to build a lifelong appreciation of the wilderness and wilderness camping.

We do not recommend bringing infants and toddlers into the BWCA. It is a wilderness and, if you have young children, we recommend camping in the established campgrounds of the Superior National Forest and state parks. They will enjoy it and it is a good preparation for BWCA camping.

School-age children can have a good experience in the BWCA if you plan activities and always consider safety first. Be sure to pick easy routes and teach them how to paddle from the bow or center of the canoe. Always ensure that children wear life vests while on the water. Practice canoeing with two or three paddlers in a canoe in calm water.

Be sure to set up age-appropriate activities for the children. For instance, while on the water, you can look for wildlife, including eagles and loons. Look for deer, moose, bear and wolves as you travel. Along the way, examine tracks, scat, and wildlife signs as well as wildflowers. Berry picking is great if you are there in the berry season, and children often enjoy fishing and collecting wood (but don't let them go alone).

Children should have a disposable camera to record their trip and take pictures of their own. You can also encourage them to listen to the sounds of nature and help them to identify the various sounds of the forest.

Rainy day activities can include coloring, reading, storytelling, and card playing. Be creative and they will enjoy the moment. Older children may enjoy journaling and taking photos.

Also inform them about the history of the region, how canoe travel was once the only way to move through the northern wilderness, and how Native Americans lived in the area and used birchbark canoes.

From our experiences with our own kids, a BWCA trip can be a very interesting and exciting experience with children if you plan well and take the time to help them enjoy it.

Fishing the BWCA

Fishing is a major part of many trips to the BWCA. Several major fish species are found in the area, including northern pike, walleyes, smallmouth bass, and a variety of trout species. As each species requires a different approach (and tackle), a brief overview can be helpful, even for experienced anglers.

Northern Pike

The northern pike fits perfectly into the northern wilderness lake. A sight-feeder, the pike attacks anything it perceives to be food or competition. Today most pike are 6 pounds or less, but you could land a trophy on any trip to the area.

FISHING TIPS: Most northerns are caught between shore and 15 feet of water. Good spots include rocky areas where dead timber emerges from the water, weed lines, and where streams and rivers enter a lake. When fishing for northerns, always use a metal leader; otherwise, the northern's sharp teeth will cut your line.

There are three basic ways to fish for northern pike: (1) anchor your canoe and use a bobber with a leech, nightcrawler, or PowerBait attached to a hook or jig; (2) let your canoe drift and use a spoon, spinner, or crankbait; (3) cast from the canoe, using spoons, spinners or crankbaits and leader.

SUGGESTED BWCA LAKES FOR NORTHERN PIKE: Brule, Juno, Pipe, Vern, Saganaga

LURE CHOICES: **Spoons:** Daredevles and spoons of varied colors; **Spinner Baits:** Try single and tandem musky spinners and buzz baits; **Surface Baits and Crankbaits:** Use large Rapalas, floating or jointed; **Jigs:** Use ⅜ oz. or larger jigs and tip with live bait or scented plastic.

Walleyes

The crown jewel of northern game fish, walleyes are an elusive challenge to catch and delicious to eat. One of the best ways to locate a school of walleyes is to use a small battery-operated fish locator and drift in your canoe until you locate fish or get a bite.

FISHING TIPS: Walleyes tend to gather in schools, so if you catch one there are likely more in the area. Walleyes are often light biters, so you may have to give them time after they tap your bait.

LIVE BAIT: When walleye fishing is tough, live bait works best. Leeches or nightcrawlers on a small jig are often effective. Slip bobbers work well when walleyes are suspended over rocks or snags. Live bait spinner rigs are also effective while drifting in a canoe.

SUGGESTED BWCA WALLEYE LAKES: Brule, Fall, Isabella, Kawishiwi, Parent

LURE CHOICES: Live Bait Rigs: Use slip/sliding sinker rigs such as "Lindy Rigs" and slip bobber rigs; **Live Bait Spinner Rigs:** Try Lindy spinner rigs of various colors; **Jigs:** Select bucktail jigs as well as painted and reflective jigs; **Crankbaits and Trolling Lures:** Try Rapala lures, including shadraps, fat Rapalas, and sinking Rapalas.

Smallmouth Bass

Smallmouth bass are pound-for-pound the hardest-fighting fish in the northland. They are, and always will be, our favorite fish on BWCA trips. A 20-inch fish is considered a trophy.

FISHING TIPS: If we could bring only one lure and live bait for smallmouth we'd bring a jig and tip it with a live leech.

Also, try slip bobbers with leeches or crawlers, as that will allow you to adjust and cast into deeper water. Our most consistent surface lure has been a chartreuse floating Rapala.

SUGGESTED BWCA SMALLMOUTH BASS LAKES: Alton, Brule, East Bearskin, Fall, Pike

LURE CHOICES: Jigs: Use bucktail jigs or small jigs with leeches, crawlers, or a plastic tail; **Spinner Baits:** Try beetle spins and Mepps spinner #1 and #2; **Top Water Lures:** Use Rapalas, either floating or jointed; **Crankbaits:** Floating Rapalas #5, #7 and #9 (chartreuse or minnow color) and Zara Spooks

Trout

Many fishermen consider trout to be the supreme freshwater fish, although they are seldom the first choice of BWCA anglers. Brook trout, rainbow trout and lake trout are found in BWCA lakes.

BWCA trout lakes tend to be very clear with good visibility. We generally use spinning tackle on these lakes with either 2- or 4-pound test line, with 6- to 8-pound line for lake trout.

FISHING TIPS FOR BROOK AND RAINBOW TROUT: We sometimes use a portable fish locator to find the trout at a certain depth and sometimes that depth is productive throughout the lake. Trout seem to roam throughout a lake as water temperature is more important than structure. Drifting or floating in your canoe using jigs or bottom-bouncing slip sinker rigs with crawlers or leeches works well for trout.

SUGGESTED LAKES FOR BROOK AND RAINBOW TROUT: Ahsub, Liz and Missing Link

LURE CHOICES: Bait Rigs: Use a Lindy rig or a sliding sinker and small hooks (Kahle or circle hooks, #8 or #10); **Jigs:** Use small jigs ($\frac{1}{64}$ oz to $\frac{1}{4}$ oz); **Spinner Lures (use a swivel):** Try Mepps #0, #1 and #2 and Panther Martin ($\frac{1}{32}$ oz. to $\frac{1}{4}$ oz.).

FISHING TIPS FOR LAKE TROUT: During late spring it is possible to find lake trout in shallow waters between 3 and 15 feet. Lures can be tipped with salted or freeze-dried minnows. Deep vertical jigging is often best in summer months. Drifting or trolling deep with a heavy sinker and a swivel attached to a spoon or plug can be productive. A good topographical map and a fish locator will help in locating lake trout.

SUGGESTED LAKES FOR LAKE TROUT: Alder, Clearwater, Jasper, Sea Gull and Tuscarora

LURE CHOICES: Jigs: ½ oz. and larger tipped with bait or twister tail; **Spoons (use swivel):** Use Doctor Spoons and trout and salmon spoons.

A Note About Tackle

Recently, many tackle manufacturers have begun producing non-lead tackle and weights. While it's not mandatory to use this gear, this tackle performs just as well as traditional tackle, and it doesn't contaminate the water or the wildlife.

Final Thoughts on BWCA Fishing

After 30 years of fishing the Boundary Waters Canoe Area we still find every trip unique and exciting. We can fish almost anywhere, but fishing in this beautiful spot is special. We've come to understand what Henry David Thoreau meant when he wrote, "Many men go fishing all of their lives without knowing that it is not fish they are after."

Suggested Equipment Checklist

The following is a list of things we have found useful to have along on our trips. You may not need all these things and you should give careful thought to what is your essential for your trip.

Basic Canoe Equipment

- ☐ BWCA entry permit
- ☐ Licensed canoe
- ☐ Seat pad or cushion
- ☐ Paddles
- ☐ Extra paddle
- ☐ Life vests
- ☐ Nylon gloves
- ☐ Anchor bag and rope
- ☐ Water bottles
- ☐ Fanny packs

Navigation

- ☐ Detailed maps
- ☐ Waterproof map case
- ☐ Compass (and spare)
- ☐ GPS (Optional)

Equipment Packs

- ☐ Large canoe packs or Duluth packs

Basic Camping Equipment

- ☐ Tent and case
- ☐ Tarps
- ☐ Bear pack and rope
- ☐ Flashlight
- ☐ Extra batteries
- ☐ Folding saw
- ☐ Pillows
- ☐ Sleeping pads
- ☐ 5 gal. water jug
- ☐ Pocket knife
- ☐ Small axe
- ☐ Extra rope
- ☐ Sleeping bags (in waterproof plastic bag)

Basic Cooking Equipment

- ☐ Cooking stove
- ☐ Fuel for stove
- ☐ Fire starter blocks
- ☐ Plates
- ☐ Silverware
- ☐ Extra zip-lock bags
- ☐ Water purifier
- ☐ Dishwashing soap
- ☐ Hot pad
- ☐ Coffee pot
- ☐ Cups
- ☐ Pots and pans
- ☐ Spatula
- ☐ Scrubbers
- ☐ Washcloths
- ☐ Boxes of waterproof matches; lighters (in each personal pack)

Clothes

- ☐ In waterproof plastic liner
- ☐ Long-sleeved shirts
- ☐ Long pants
- ☐ Socks
- ☐ Shorts
- ☐ T-Shirt
- ☐ Swimsuit
- ☐ Underwear
- ☐ Hat
- ☐ Shoes or boots (two pairs)
- ☐ Water shoes
- ☐ Sunglasses
- ☐ Rain suit or poncho

Personal Hygiene

- ☐ Toothbrush
- ☐ Toothpaste
- ☐ Toilet paper
- ☐ Hand soap
- ☐ Towel
- ☐ Shampoo
- ☐ Insect repellent
- ☐ Sunscreen
- ☐ Lip balm
- ☐ Fingernail clipper
- ☐ Imodium
- ☐ First aid kit

Miscellaneous

- ☐ Small folding saw
- ☐ Extra batteries
- ☐ Garbage bags
- ☐ Duct tape
- ☐ Reading material
- ☐ Playing cards
- ☐ Small camera
- ☐ Extra batteries for digital camera
- ☐ Extra memory card for digital camera

Fishing Equipment

- ☐ Fishing license
- ☐ Tackle box
- ☐ Favorite lures
- ☐ Leeches or crawlers
- ☐ Depth finder
- ☐ Bait containers
- ☐ Landing net
- ☐ Stringer
- ☐ Fillet knife
- ☐ Collapsible or sectional fishing poles

If you don't have all the camping or paddling gear you need, or you want to rent a canoe for your trip to the BWCA, there are many outfitters in the BWCA where you can rent equipment. For an up-to-date listing of the outfitters that operate in each portion of the BWCA, visit the following websites.

Western Area: The Ely Chamber of Commerce, www.ely.org

Central Area: The Lutsen-Tofte Tourism Association, www.co.cook.mn.us/index.php/visiting/tourism/lutsen-tofte-tourism-association

Eastern Area: The Gunflint Trail Association, www.gunflint-trail.com

How to Use this Book

The BWCA covers over a million acres of land, and there are entry points scattered throughout. The 20 trips in this book are divided into three sections: west, central and east. Our driving directions begin from Ely in the western section, Tofte in the central section and Grand Marais in the eastern section.

Trip Highlights, Campsites and Day Trips

In the account of each trip, we start out by telling you why we like it, including notable highlights. For each, we list a campsite we'd recommend, and we provide directions to that campsite from the entry point. Sometimes this requires portaging and paddling; sometimes it simply requires paddling. If the campsite we recommend is already occupied, we list alternate sites. Whichever site you choose, we recommend that you base camp—stay at this camp each night and use it as your hub of operations. We also offer a list of optional day trips. These often involve trips to other lakes or notable sites, and sometimes include portages or hikes. These portages are optional, and we've specified this in the text. "Required portages" are portages you must take to reach our recommended campsite. (Portages are not required for all of the trips in this book; some lakes are specified in the text as drop-in lakes, where you simply park your car at the boat launch, unload your gear, and paddle to your campsite.)

What to Know before You Go

To help you plan your trip, we've specified some of the details about each trip. We rate the trip in terms of difficulty, include the commercial maps that pertain to the area, list how many campsites are available and how many daily permits are allowed for the entry point, and we recommend how many days to stay. With all this information in hand, you should be ready to go!

West Area Trips

West Area Trips

Ely, Minnesota, is the gateway to the entry points of the western and south-western lakes of the BWCA. Once referred to as "the nation's playground," Ely is a wonderful place to visit. In fact, Arthur Frommer's *Budget Travel* magazine recently selected Ely as the "coolest small town in America." Ely's end-of-the-road location and proximity to the BWCA was a big part of the selection. Some of the more popular western entry points to the BWCA are located near Ely, especially those along the Echo Trail and Fernberg Road.

Table of Contents

Little Indian Sioux River (North) - Entry Point 14 46

Mudro Lake - Entry Point 23 52

Fall Lake - Entry Point 24. 58

Wood Lake - Entry Point 26 64

Snowbank Lake - Entry Point 27 70

Lake One - Entry Point 30 76

Hegman Lake - Entry Point 77 82

Entry Point 14-Little Indian Sioux River (North)

Devil's Cascade

Why We Like This Trip

Located north of Ely on the Echo Trail, the Little Indian Sioux River (North) provides a varied and serene BWCA experience. This trip, which begins on a river, also provides access to the famous Devil's Cascade, a series of rapids and waterfalls that descends 75 feet. Wildlife, especially turtles, beavers, loons and deer are plentiful and a moose sighting cannot be ruled out. You may also see bear. The river empties into Upper Pauness Lake; you can camp at one of the five campsites and take day trips from there, or you can take the 40-rod portage to Lower Pauness Lake, another beautiful BWCA lake.

HIGHLIGHTS

- This is a complete BWCA experience, where you'll travel the famous Echo Trail, paddle on a wilderness river, carry your canoe over moderate portages and let the beauty of the BWCA surround you.

- See the Devil's Cascade, a majestic and powerful series of rapids and waterfalls that descends over 75 feet as the Little Indian Sioux continues its journey north.

Getting From the Entry Point to the Campsite

From the entry point, you start with a 40-rod portage to the river. After paddling about 2.5 miles on this winding river (about 45 minutes) you will come to a 65-rod portage around some lovely rapids. As you leave this portage, you will see an interesting rocky outcrop to your left where Jeanette Creek enters the Little Sioux. The water levels here are set by season (heavy in spring, almost nonexistent in late summer). Continue winding for another 2.25 miles (about an hour) and you will enter Upper Pauness Lake, a small but beautiful and tranquil BWCA lake. You then paddle to a portage, which is on the east side of the lake and leads to Lower Pauness Lake. Take this 40-rod portage, and then head north (left) about 0.5 miles to the campsite. This is a lovely elevated campsite, with a view of Lower Pauness Lake entering the Devil's Cascade. This campsite has some great tent sites.

Selecting a Campsite

If the site just before the cascade is taken, you have two options, an easy one and a hard one. The easy one is to cross to the east bank of Lower Pauness to the southeast for a little under 0.5 miles and take the good site there. The

Entry Point 14-Little Indian Sioux River (North)

hard choice is to make the steep and somewhat difficult 110-rod portage to the campsite at the far end of the Devil's Cascade. It is a nice site but difficult to reach. If you do choose this site, we recommend that you hike it first to make sure it is open to avoid having to backtrack with your gear.

While You're There/Day Trip:

DAY TRIP 1. Be sure to visit the Devil's Cascade, which is located at the north end of Lower Pauness. This is a long, raging stretch of rapids that makes for many good pictures. Side trails allow you to get very close to these rapids and get good views of the fast-moving water. Just be careful not to lose your footing. You can portage or hike the full 110 rods alongside these rapids.

DAY TRIP 2. If you are healthy and the adventurous type, you may chose to carry your canoe over the Devil's Cascade portage, a very difficult portage that includes an 80-foot hill. After the portage, you can explore the Little Indian Sioux River all the way to Loon Lake, which is approximately 2 miles away.

Devil's Cascade

DAY TRIP 3. The 216-rod portage to Shell Lake on the east side of Lower Pauness Lake makes a nice hike. You may choose to carry your canoe over this portage for some fishing on Shell Lake. Be sure to bring insect repellent and a camera.

PORTAGES TO GET TO CAMPSITE: 3, a 40-rod portage from the parking lot to Little Indian Sioux River, a 65-rod portage on Little Indian Sioux and a 40-rod portage to Lower Pauness Lake

OPTIONAL PORTAGES (DAY TRIPS/HIKES): 1 portage to the Devil's Cascade (110 rods); 1 portage to reach Shell Lake (216 rods)

DIFFICULTY: Easy to moderate

CAMPSITES: 4 on Upper Pauness and 3 on Lower Pauness

DAILY QUOTA: 6

SUGGESTED NUMBER OF DAYS: 3–5

Lower Pauness Campsite

Entry Point 14-Little Indian Sioux River (North)

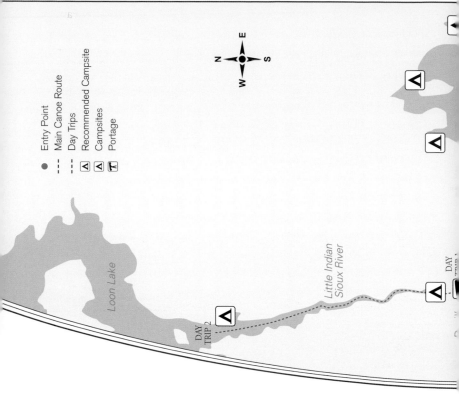

Directions to Entry Point:

About 0.5 miles east of Ely, turn left on County Road 88. Take this for about 2 miles until you come to the Echo Trail (there is a small sign). Turn right onto the Echo Trail (County 116). Now take this road for about 29 miles until you cross Little Indian Sioux Creek. Take an immediate right into the parking lot and entry point. Note: Make sure you are in the Little Indian Sioux North lot as there is also a Little Indian Sioux South lot. The total distance from Ely to this entry point is 32 miles.

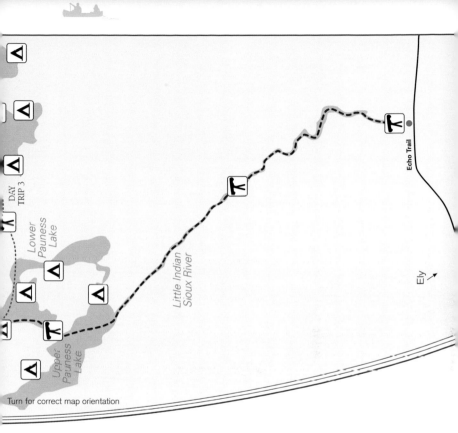

DAY
TRIP 3

Lower
Pauness
Lake

Little Indian
Sioux River

Echo Trail

Ely

Upper
Pauness
Lake

Turn for correct map orientation

Things to Know Before You Go:

Maps: McKenzie maps 12 and 14; Fisher map 16; Voyageur map 1

Longitude/Latitude: North 48° 02' 45"; West 91° 55' 13"

Contact/Outfitters: Ely area outfitters

Lake Names: Upper Pauness, Lower Pauness, Loon, Shell

Entry Point 23–Mudro Lake

End of 2nd
Fourtown portage

Why We Like This Trip

In the past, the Mudro entry point was famous because it was the location of the Chainsaw Sisters Saloon. Unfortunately, the saloon is now gone. Despite this, Mudro provides an excellent base-camp lake because of the many opportunities it provides for day trips to other lakes. It's also an excellent choice for those starting their journey later in the day and those who do not want to engage in a long initial paddle. It is a charming, small lake reached after about 1 mile of paddling down a winding, slow-moving river (about half an hour). There are many turtles and loons on this river and we were surprised we did not see any deer. Mudro has some very good fishing, especially for walleyes and northern pike. There is only

HIGHLIGHTS

- The 125-rod portage between Mudro Lake and Fourtown Lake is spectacular as it climbs through a scenic canyon; it makes a great day hike.

- Mudro Lake connects to nearby Fourtown Lake, an excellent fishing destination for anglers seeking walleyes, northerns and smallmouth bass.

one campsite on this lake but we seldom saw it used even though it is a good campsite, and it does not require much time and effort to get to it. Be aware that Mudro is on the main route for people heading up to Fourtown Lake and to House Lake and Basswood. Consequently, expect to see other canoes on the lake.

Getting From the Entry Point to the Campsite

There is a very easy 30-rod portage from the entry point to the river. After going down the river and entering the lake, head just northeast for 0.75 miles to the opposite side of the lake and locate the only campsite on the lake. It is easy to see, and it has good views and elevation.

Selecting a Campsite

We recommend the lone campsite on Mudro, but if it is taken, keep the shoreline on your left and head east for about 0.5 miles until you come to the portage to Sandpit Lake. This is an 83-rod portage that is somewhat difficult due to all the rocks on the portage. Watch your feet as you walk it. Once you reach Sandpit Lake, there is a good campsite about 0.5 miles on the northern side of the lake. (Keep the landmass on your left.) As on Mudro, we seldom saw people using this perfectly good campsite.

Entry Point 23-Mudro Lake

While You're There/Day Trip:

DAY TRIP 1. A day trip from Mudro Lake to Fourtown Lake features a set of three interesting but somewhat difficult portages through a beautiful, high-walled gorge. At the northernmost point of Mudro Lake, there is a small channel that leads to Fourtown Lake. The first portage on the right bank is only 34 rods but it is rocky and can be slippery. The second portage of 125 rods is on the left bank and follows a rocky and elevated path along the gorge. The views are spectacular and more enjoyable if you're not carrying a pack or a canoe, making this a good choice for a day trip. The last portage into Fourtown is around a rapids and is on the right side, and it is 15 rods long. Fishermen may wish to carry a canoe across Fourtown, where the fishing can be very good.

DAY TRIP 2. The trip from Mudro Lake to Tin Can Mike Lake is good for fishing and exploring. There are two portages involved, and 2.25 miles of paddling. The first portage of 83 rods takes you from Mudro Lake to Sandpit Lake and is

Fourtown Portage rocks

fairly rugged, rocky and has some large hills. The portage from Sandpit Lake to Tin Can Mike Lake is 135 rods and is easier than the previous portage. Tin Can Mike has good fishing for walleyes, northerns and bluegills. The first campsite halfway up on the western side of Tin Can Mike is a good place for a lunch break. After that, reverse your route and return to your tent site. Spend a relaxed day on Mudro fishing walleyes or northerns, exploring and taking pictures. Our best loon pictures came from Mudro.

PORTAGES TO GET TO CAMPSITE: 1, an easy 30-rod portage from the parking lot to the river leading into Mudro Lake

OPTIONAL PORTAGES (DAY TRIPS/HIKES): 3 optional portages are required to reach Fourtown Lake (34 rods, 125 rods, 15 rods); 2 optional portages are required to reach Tin Can Mike (83 rods, 135 rods)

DIFFICULTY: Moderately difficult as the portages are rocky and hilly

CAMPSITES: 1 Mudro, 1 Sandpit, 3 Tin Can Mike, 14 Fourtown

DAILY QUOTA: 7—this is a very popular entry point

SUGGESTED NUMBER OF DAYS: 1 day in, 1 day out, 3 days to fish and day-trip

Painted turtle

Entry Point 23-Mudro Lake

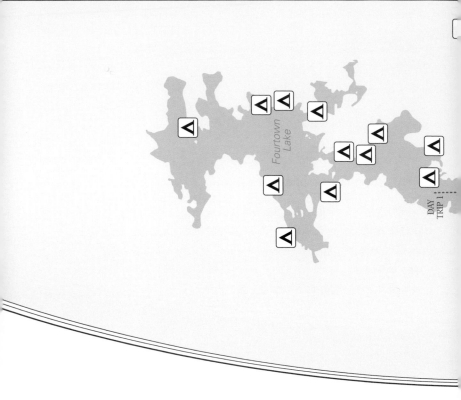

Directions to Entry Point:

About 0.5 miles east of Ely, turn left on County Road 88. Take this for about 2 miles until you come to the Echo Trail (County 116); look for the small sign. Turn right onto the Echo Trail. Now take this road for about 13 miles, this will lead past two entrances to Fenske Lake. Just past the second of these is a small Mudro Lake sign and you turn right on this road. You will immediately come to a "Y." Keep to the left and drive about 3 miles to the parking lot. The total distance from Ely to the entry point is 19 miles.

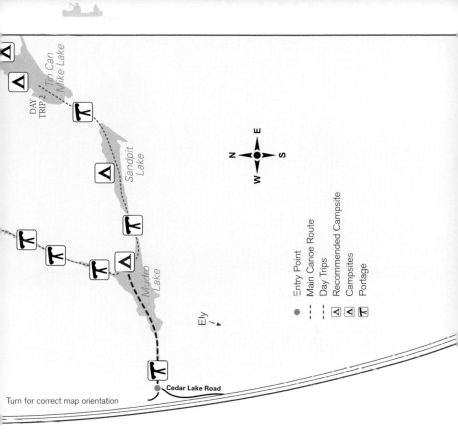

Turn for correct map orientation

Things to Know Before You Go:

  Maps: Fisher map 9; McKenzie map 11; Voyageur map 4
  Longitude/Latitude: North 48° 02' 3"; West 41° 55' 13"
  Contact/Outfitters: Ely area outfitters
  Lake Names: Mudro, Sandpit, Tin Can Mike, Fourtown

Entry Point 24–Fall Lake

Start of Newton Falls

Why We Like This Trip

Fall Lake is located next to a Superior National Forest campground where you can stay the night before you enter. This is the most modern campground in the Superior National Forest. It has electricity, showers, indoor toilets, as well as a nice swimming beach. This trip is an excellent choice for a first trip to the BWCA with a family. Fall Lake is also a drop-in lake with no portage required. Note that Fall Lake is open to motors of up to 25 horsepower, so it has less of a wilderness feel to it and should be avoided by those who want a motor-free experience. On the other hand, it also has some of the nicest sandy beach campsites in the BWCA. The fishing is also usually very good, especially for walleyes and small-

mouth bass. Finally, this was the only lake where we saw a bald eagle's nest on our trip, and there was an eaglet in this nest.

Getting From the Entry Point to the Campsite

From the entry point, paddle north less than 0.5 miles and you will see Mile Island ahead of you. This island has six campsites, some with beautiful beaches, and you can paddle around the island until you find one that is open. We'd recommend any of these sites.

Selecting a Campsite

If all the Mile Island campsites are taken, two other good ones are located very near Newton Falls. To get to these, once you have passed the southwest tip of Mile Island, keep the mainland on your left for a little over 1 mile and you will come to the first one, almost where the Newton Falls portage begins. The other one is less than 0.25 miles east of the Newton Falls portage.

While You're There/Day Trip:

DAY TRIP 1. Fall Lake also features some good day-trip options, including a trip to two picturesque rapids, Newton Falls and Pipestone Falls on Basswood

Entry Point 24–Fall Lake

Lake. This trip features two smooth, wide and easy portages. Portage wheels are allowed on these portages as well as motors and boats. To reach Newton Falls, start from Mile Island, and paddle north toward Newton Lake and take the Newton Falls portage. This is an easy portage of 80 rods and travels around the falls' rapids, and good photos are possible here. After completing the portage, head north until you reach the northern end of Newton Lake and the second portage. The second portage is 80 rods and takes you around Pipestone Falls and into Pipestone Bay on beautiful and historic Basswood Lake. While you are on this day trip, you should be on the lookout for bald eagles. Some campers may wish to hike one or both of the two portages, depending on where their base camp is. The falls and portages make interesting photos, and if you complete the Pipestone Falls Portage you can also photograph Basswood Lake.

Fall Lake vista

DAY TRIP 2. In addition, if you camp on Mile Island, be sure to paddle and fish around the island. You can also explore the northern reaches of Fall Lake and its bays. No portaging is required for these day trips.

PORTAGES TO GET TO CAMPSITE: None, this is a drop-in lake

OPTIONAL PORTAGES (DAY TRIPS/HIKES): There is 1 portage from Fall Lake around Newton Falls to Newton Lake (80 rods); there is 1 portage from Newton Lake around Pipestone Falls to Basswood Lake's Pipestone Bay (80 rods)

DIFFICULTY: Easy, though wind on Fall Lake and Basswood Lake should be considered, as it sometimes poses a dangerous challenge

CAMPSITES: 8 on Fall, 2 on Newton

DAILY QUOTA: 14

SUGGESTED NUMBER OF DAYS: 3–5

Newton portage end and Newton Lake

Entry Point 24–Fall Lake

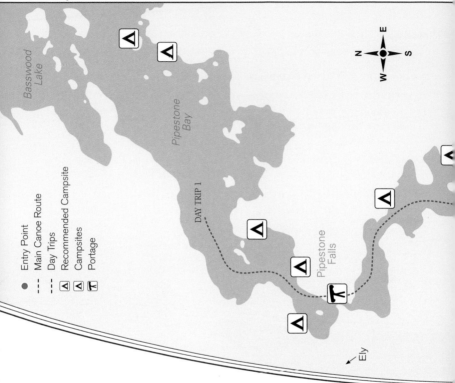

Directions to Entry Point:

From Ely, take MN-169 east for about 2.5 miles. This will take you to Winton. About 1 mile east of Winton, MN-169 ends and Fernberg Road begins (County Road 18). On Fernberg Road, drive east for about 3 miles and look for the Fall Lake sign. Turn left onto Fall Lake Road (County Road 182) and drive about 1 mile to the Fall Lake Campground and public landing. The total distance from Ely to the entry point is about 7 miles.

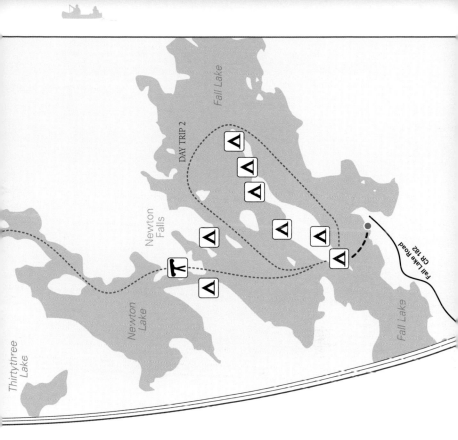

Things to Know Before You Go:

   Maps: Fisher map 10; McKenzie map 17; Voyageur map 4
   Longitude/Latitude: North 47° 57' 9"; West 91° 43' 16"
   Contact/Outfitters: Ely area outfitters
   Lake Names: Fall, Newton, Basswood

Entry Point 26–Wood Lake

Wood Lake from
Hula Portage

Why We Like This Trip

Because of the long, 180-rod portage that leads to the lake, Wood Lake is much
less crowded than most BWCA Lakes and provides an excellent place for solitude
and gives you a true alone-in-the-wilderness feel. It is an excellent fishing lake with
abundant walleyes and smallmouth bass. Wood Lake is also an excellent place to
see wildlife. On our most recent trip, we saw several bald eagles, many loons, and
were surprised that we didn't see moose in the shallow, grassy areas. Wood Lake
may look simple on a map but be sure to bring a compass and map along, as the
peninsulas and islands can throw off your navigation and get you lost.

HIGHLIGHTS

- Wood Lake is less crowded than other entry points and has a true wilderness feel. The 180-rod portage into Wood Lake keeps many away, but it is fairly flat and slopes slightly downhill toward the lake.

- Wood Lake also connects with several less-traveled small lakes as well as historic Basswood Lake.

Getting From the Entry Point to the Campsite

As noted, there is a 180-rod portage from the entry point to the lake. The lake is very narrow when you enter it, but it quickly opens up. There are five campsites on this lake, and the one we prefer is on a peninsula about 0.75 miles northwest from the entry point. As you paddle to this site, you will encounter an island. Keep to the left of this island and continue heading north until you come to the campsite on a peninsula on your left. It is a good, elevated site with good views in three directions.

Selecting a Campsite

If the peninsula site is occupied, there is another good site about 0.5 miles to the northwest of it. Alternatively, if you want to be closer to the Hula portage into Hula Lake, you can keep the mainland on your right and continue paddling north for about 0.75 miles to another good site on the north side of the mainland along a somewhat narrow channel.

While You're There/Day Trip:

Wood Lake is a very good fishing lake for walleyes and smallmouth bass and you should spend a day fishing the bays and rocky areas of the lake.

Entry Point 26-Wood Lake

Fishing can be good all over Wood Lake, but we tend to fish the northern and northeastern bays and the shoreline.

DAY TRIP 1. If you like exploring, you may consider paddling the approximately 2 miles from the preferred campsite to the Hula Portage (51 rods) and paddle 1.75 miles on shallow Hula Lake to the portage to Good Lake (150 rods), which is located in the northwest bay of Good Lake. You will paddle north and slightly west for about 0.5 miles to the tip of a small bay, where an 85-rod portage leads to Basswood's Hoist Bay. Some may choose to hike this portage without a canoe to photograph historic Basswood Lake. If you choose to carry your canoe to Basswood, always be aware of wind and waves, as Basswood can be very rough in the wind. Be sure to bring good maps and a compass with you. Reverse your route to return to your campsite.

Wood Lake rocky shore

DAY TRIP 2. A day trip for fishing on Good Lake for walleyes, northerns and smallmouths can also be rewarding. Hula has some northerns, but we prefer Good Lake.

PORTAGES TO GET TO CAMPSITE: 1, an initial 180-rod portage that discourages some people, but it is fairly flat and slopes slightly downhill toward the lake; the portage isn't a problem if you take your time; many will double portage this entry point

OPTIONAL PORTAGES (DAY TRIPS/HIKES): The portage from Wood Lake to Hula Lake is 51 rods; the portage from Hula Lake to Good Lake is 150 rods; the portage from Good Lake to Basswood Lake's Hoist Bay is 85 rods

DIFFICULTY: Moderate, due to the long, but not difficult, 180-rod portage to Wood Lake at the entry point

CAMPSITES: 4 on Wood Lake

DAILY QUOTA: 2

SUGGESTED NUMBER OF DAYS: 1 day in, 1 day out, 2 or 3 days fishing and exploring

Wood Lake entrance

Entry Point 26–Wood Lake

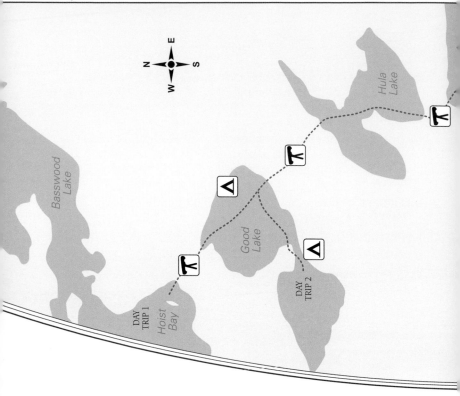

Directions to Entry Point:

From Ely, take MN-169 east for about 2.5 miles, this will lead you to Winton. About 1 mile east of Winton, MN-169 ends and Fernberg Road begins (County Road 18). On Fernberg Road, drive east for about 9 miles and look for the Wood Lake sign and turn left. Take this road about 0.25 miles to the parking lot. The total distance from Ely to the entry point is about 13 miles.

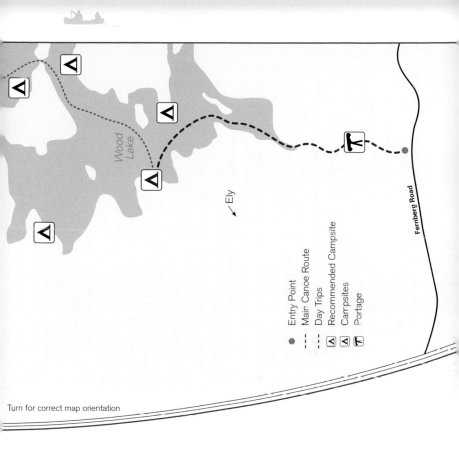

Wood Lake

← Ely

Fernberg Road

Entry Point
Main Canoe Route
Day Trips
Recommended Campsite
Campsites
Portage

Turn for correct map orientation

Things to Know Before You Go:

Maps: Fisher maps 10 and 31; McKenzie map 17; Voyageur map 4

Longitude/Latitude: North 47° 57' 31"; West 91° 36' 15"

Contact/Outfitters: Ely area outfitters

Lake Names: Wood, Hula, Good, Basswood

Entry Point 27-Snowbank Lake

Snowbank islands

Why We Like This Trip

Snowbank Lake is a very large lake of 4,273 acres and it is one of the clearest lakes in the entire BWCA, with a clarity level of 23 feet. It has many islands and beautiful vistas and is one of the best lakes in the BWCA for fishing for lake trout. Snowbank also has some good, spacious campsites. The lake's western and southern portions are not part of the BWCA and can therefore be used by motorboats, but avoiding motorboats is fairly easy. To do so, simply paddle east from the entry point for about 0.75 miles; this will take you into the BWCA and you will not see another motorboat. From Snowbank Lake, you can also easily portage into several other lakes that are completely within the BWCA, and the lake provides access to an excellent loop

day trip. Be sure to take wind into consideration, however, as inclement weather can develop quickly here.

Getting From the Entry Point to the Campsite

Snowbank Lake is a drop-in lake, meaning that you can unload your vehicle right at the entry point without an initial portage. From this entry point, we recommend that you paddle about 0.5 miles east and just north of Burnt Island. Then head southeast for about 0.75 miles to the Parent Lake portage. Cross this 40-rod portage and enter Parent Lake. There is a very nice, protected campsite about 0.5 miles to your left. We recommend camping there.

Selecting a Campsite

As we noted above, the best campsite is on Parent Lake. If this campsite is taken, continue with the mainland on your left for another 0.5 miles where there is another good site. If this is also taken, paddle another 0.25 miles to the Disappointment Lake portage and take this 40-rod portage. Once you enter Disappointment Lake, there is a nice site about 0.5 miles to your right and there are nine other sites on this lake. Check your map for their locations.

Entry Point 27–Snowbank Lake

While You're There/Day Trip:

Consider a day of fishing on Snowbank for smallmouth bass, walleyes and particularly lake trout. If you fish for lake trout, you will need a trout stamp on your fishing license. Try fishing near the islands, and keep in mind that lake trout seek deeper water as the year warms up. If you prefer fishing smaller lakes, fish Parent Lake for walleyes and smallmouth. Disappointment Lake is long and narrow, but it also has walleyes and smallmouth bass. If it's windy, try these smaller lakes.

DAY TRIP 1. Some of you may like to try a loop route; if so, we recommend the following route: From your campsite on Parent Lake, paddle to the north end of Parent to the 80-rod portage to Disappointment Lake. As you reach Disappointment Lake, the trail heads off to your left and there is a 140-rod portage to Snowbank Lake. Once on Snowbank, keep the mainland on your left as you head west and then south along the shore. This will bring you

Snowbank vista

back to Wilderness Bay and the 40-rod portage to Parent Lake, which is the original portage you used to enter Parent Lake Once over the portage you can return to your campsite on Parent Lake. A loop trip is more fun with a canoe and no heavy portage packs.

PORTAGES TO GET TO CAMPSITE: 1, a 40-rod portage from Snowbank Lake into Parent Lake, but no portages are required to stay on Snowbank Lake

OPTIONAL PORTAGES (DAY TRIPS/HIKES): If you take the loop route, there are 3 optional portages, from Parent to Disappointment Lake (80 rods), from Disappointment Lake to Snowbank (140 rods), and from Snowbank to Parent (40 rods)

DIFFICULTY: Easy, but be aware of the wind on Snowbank Lake

CAMPSITES: 2 on Parent, 12 on Disappointment Lake

DAILY QUOTA: 8

SUGGESTED NUMBER OF DAYS: 1 day in, 1 day out, 2–3 days at campsite

Snowbank islands

Entry Point 27-Snowbank Lake

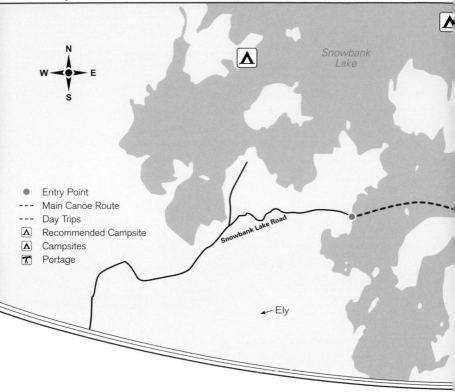

Snowbank Lake

- ●   Entry Point
- ---   Main Canoe Route
- ---   Day Trips
- △   Recommended Campsite
- △   Campsites
- ⛵   Portage

Snowbank Lake Road

← Ely

Directions to Entry Point:

From Ely, take MN-169 east for about 2.5 miles. This will lead you to Winton. About 1 mile east of Winton, MN-169 ends and Fernberg Road (County Road 18) begins. On Fernberg Road, drive east for about 19 miles and look for the sign for Snowbank Lake. Turn left and you will be on Snowbank Road. Take this road for about 2 miles until you come to a "Y." Take the right fork for about 1.5 miles; this leads to the public landing and parking lot. The total distance from Ely to the entry point is 24 miles.

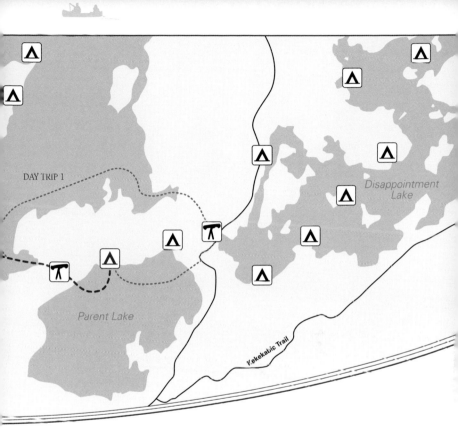

DAY TRIP 1

Disappointment Lake

Parent Lake

Kekekabic Trail

Things to Know Before You Go:

   Maps: Fisher map 11; McKenzie map 9; Voyageur map 7
   Longitude/Latitude: North 48° 01' 59"; West 91° 55' 32"
   Contact/Outfitters: Ely area outfitters
   Lake Names: Snowbank, Disappointment, Parent

Entry Point 30–Lake One

Channel on Lake One

Why We Like This Trip

If you look at a map, Lake One looks to be a fairly large lake, and it is. But it certainly doesn't feel like one. Instead, it's more of an abundance of small lakes held together by the channels that run between all the islands. Maybe that's why it is such a popular lake. We think it should really be called Island Lake, as there are so many passages and islands to explore. We spent two full days there just paddling around to see what was around the next bend. Another advantage to Lake One is that it has many good campsites. Be aware that it is easy to get lost on Lake One amid all the islands and peninsulas, and note that many of the islands are not indicated on

maps. Visitors need good map reading skills, a good compass, and a good map (for this lake we strongly recommend the highly detailed McKenzie map). Always try to know where the mainland is and keep it constantly on one side of your canoe heading in, and on the other side when headed out.

Getting From the Entry Point to the Campsite

Lake One is a drop-in lake with no portage required to enter. Once your canoe is loaded, head to your left (east) to a point on the opposite side of the channel. Continue east, crossing a small bay on your right to the opposite shore and follow it northeast until you come to a very small opening. The total distance here is about 0.5 miles (15 minutes). Enter this narrow channel and follow it for about 0.25 miles (less than 15 minutes). You will then come into a much larger channel going north and south. To the north, on your left, is Kawishiwi Outfitters but you want to turn right (south) into this larger channel, keeping the main landmass on your right for a little over 1 mile. You'll pass a small bay on your right; at the southwestern point of this bay, cross to the other side of the channel and you will find an excellent campsite that has good tent sites and is elevated, with good views in three directions.

Entry Point 30-Lake One

Selecting a Campsite

As mentioned above, Lake One's campsites are its real virtues; in all, there are 12 campsites on the lake. If the recommended campsite is in use, we suggest you paddle about 0.5 miles southwest to an island where there are two nice campsites. If these are taken, another good campsite is located about 0.25 miles northwest on the mainland.

While You're There/Day Trip:

We like spending the bulk of our time on Lake One, as it involves no portages. Most campers on Lake One will find more than enough to do as they explore the islands, bays and shoreline. Always be sure to take a map and compass with you when you day-trip.

Small island on Lake One

DAY TRIP 1. If you want to portage, you can take the two relatively easy portages to Lake Two. The first is 30 rods long, and the second is 40 rods. You can take pictures, fish, and berry pick along the way.

PORTAGES TO GET TO CAMPSITE: No portages required to stay on Lake One

OPTIONAL PORTAGES (DAY TRIPS/HIKES): 2 optional portages to reach Lake Two, the first is 30 rods and the second is 40 rods

DIFFICULTY: Easy—no portages are required if you camp on Lake One

CAMPSITES: 12 on Lake One, 12 on Lake Two

DAILY QUOTA: 30

SUGGESTED NUMBER OF DAYS: We like a 4-day trip to Lake One; 1 day in, 1 day out, and 2 days to fish and explore

Lake One campsite

Entry Point 30–Lake One

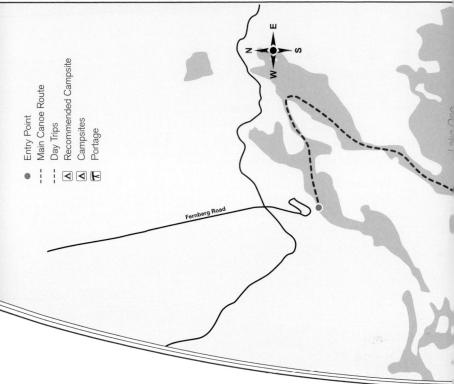

Directions to Entry Point:

From Ely, take MN-169 east for about 2.5 miles to Winton. About 1 mile east of Winton, MN-169 ends and Fernberg Road (County Road 18) begins. On Fernberg Road, drive east for about 23 miles and look for the Lake One sign on your right. The total distance from Ely to the entry point is about 26 miles. If you're planning on renting equipment from Kawishiwi Outfitters, watch for a sign on the left side of the road just before the entry point. You can park just past this sign and drop your canoe in at the public landing.

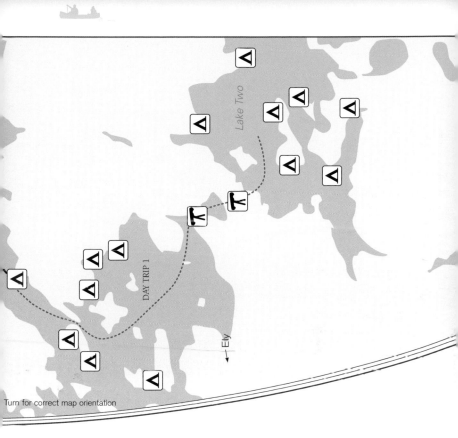

Turn for correct map orientation

Things to Know Before You Go:

Maps: Fisher maps 3, 10, and 31; McKenzie map 9 and 18; Voyageur map 7

Longitude/Latitude: North 47° 58' 22"; West 91° 28' 42"

Contact/Outfitters: Ely area outfitters

Lake Names: Lake One, Lake Two

Entry Point 77–Hegman Lake

Landing at South Hegman Lake

Why We Like This Trip

What is often referred to as Hegman Lake is really two lakes, North Hegman Lake and South Hegman Lake. Both are small, beautiful lakes. The reason they get lumped together is that only a short, 6-rod portage separates them. They are most famous for the very old Native American pictographs on North Hegman Lake. These are the best pictographs in the BWCA area and people have speculated for years what they mean and who made them. While visiting, you can conjure up your own interpretations. Both North and South Hegman provide good smallmouth fishing, and the scenic beauty and serenity, especially

on South Hegman, are superb. In late July and August, there is also excellent blueberry picking on many open hillsides.

Getting From the Entry Point to the Campsite

From the entry point, there is an easy 80-rod portage to South Hegman Lake. Once on the lake, if you keep the mainland on your right for about 0.5 miles (about half an hour), you will come to a point with an excellent campsite. It has very nice tent sites, is elevated several feet above the waterline, and provides excellent vistas of the lake in several directions. If this campsite is taken, two other very good ones exist on South Hegman (there are none on North Hegman). One of these is directly north from the site on the point. The other is east-southeast on the eastern end of a bay.

Selecting a Campsite

We suggest one of the three good campsites on South Hegman. However, if these are all taken, paddle into North Hegman and take the 153-rod portage to Little Bass Lake, another lovely little lake that has three good, but seldom-used, campsites about 0.75 miles from the portage on the northeastern part of this lake.

Entry Point 77–Hegman Lake

While You're There/Day Trip:

You may want to try blueberry picking on the flat rocks of the northeast bay of South Hegman when berries are in season. Also, try fishing the sunken trees and shorelines with floating lures for smallmouth bass in the morning and evening. If you have live leeches, they work well for smallmouth and walleyes.

DAY TRIP 1. After you've set up your base camp, most campers will be anxious to see the famous Hegman Pictographs on North Hegman Lake. To get there, paddle from your campsite to the north shore of South Hegman Lake and take the very short and easy 6-rod portage into North Hegman. The pictographs are estimated to be at least 500 years old; they are well preserved on the side of a cliff at the north end of North Hegman Lake. You will want your camera on this interesting trip. If you are late in setting up your camp you may want to wait for another day when you can spend time at the pictographs and explore or fish North Hegman and nearby Trease Lake.

Hegman Lake kayaker

DAY TRIP 2. For more fishing, you can take the 153-rod portage on the southeast corner of North Hegman into Little Bass Lake. It's a fairly steep climb over a hill, but the fishing for smallmouth bass can be excellent.

PORTAGES TO GET TO CAMPSITE: 1, an 80-rod portage from the parking lot (at the end, there is a stairway that descends to the shore of South Hegman Lake)

OPTIONAL PORTAGES (DAY TRIPS/HIKES): To visit the famous Hegman Pictographs, there is a 6-rod portage from South Hegman Lake to North Hegman Lake; to reach Little Bass Lake from North Hegman, there is a 153-rod portage

DIFFICULTY: Easy

CAMPSITES: 3 on South Hegman, 3 on Little Bass

DAILY QUOTA: 2

SUGGESTED NUMBER OF DAYS: 5; 1 day in, 1 day out, 2 days day-tripping, fishing and exploring

Hegman Lake campsite

Entry Point 77-Hegman Lake

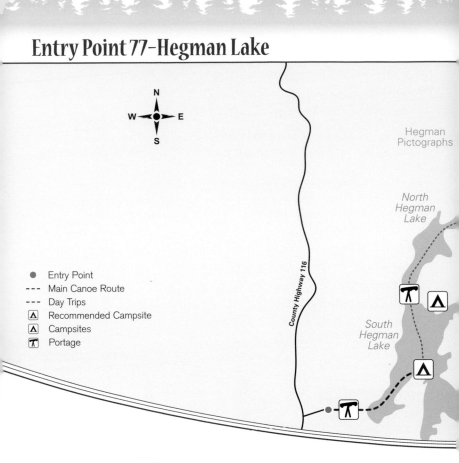

Directions to Entry Point:

About 0.5 miles east of Ely, turn left on County Road 88. Take this for about 2 miles until you come to the Echo Trail (County 116). (There is a small sign.) Turn right onto the Echo Trail. Now take this road for about 13 miles. A little under 1 mile after you pass First Lake you should see a turn to the right for South Hegman Lake. After turning right, drive about 0.25 miles and enter the parking lot. The total distance from Ely to the entry point is 16 miles.

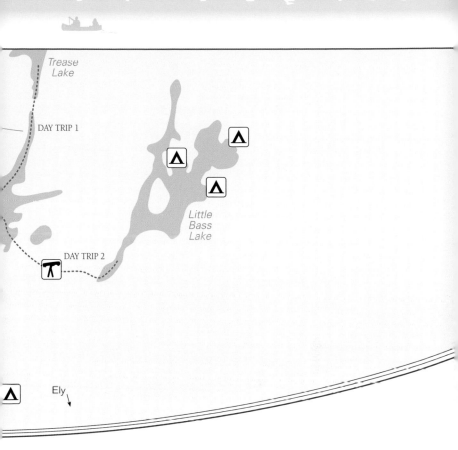

Trease
Lake

DAY TRIP 1

Little
Bass
Lake

DAY TRIP 2

Ely

Things to Know Before You Go:

Maps: Fisher map 9; McKenzie map 11; Voyageur map 3

Longitude/Latitude: North 48° 01' 59"; West 91° 55' 32"

Contact/Outfitters: Ely area outfitters

Lake Names: South Hegman, North Hegman, Trease, Little Bass

Central Area Trips

Central Area Trips

Tofte is a very small town on the shore of Lake Superior. Originally
founded as a fishing village, it now serves as the main gateway to the lakes
in the central portion of the BWCA. County Road 2, also known as the
Sawbill Trail, is just a mile north of Tofte and leads to the entry points of
many lakes in the central area of the BWCA.

Table of Contents

Isabella - Entry Point 35 90

Hog Creek - Entry Point 36 96

Kawishiwi Lake - Entry Point 37 102

Sawbill Lake - Entry Point 38 108

Baker Lake - Entry Point 39 114

Homer Lake - Entry Point 40 120

Brule Lake - Entry Point 41 126

Entry Point 35-Isabella Lake

Bird Island

Why We Like This Trip

Isabella Lake is a remote entry point that doesn't receive much traffic, giving it a true wilderness feel. The entry point is located on the site of an old lumber town that flourished from 1949 to 1964. It is gone now and the forest has reclaimed the area, but some artifacts are occasionally found in this area. Isabella Lake is a medium-sized lake with excellent fishing, especially for walleyes, northerns and smallmouth bass. There are ten good campsites, including three island sites, so the likelihood of finding an open site is very good. There are also some interesting rivers on the west side of the lake to explore and one of these,

- This is a remote entry point that feels like wilderness almost immediately. The lake features 11 very nice campsites that are rarely used; you should have no trouble finding a great site. These sites provide great opportunities to explore this lake.

- From Isabella Lake's western shore, you can follow river channels and connect with the scenic Island River.

with a 28-rod portage, provides access to the Pow Wow Trail. The Pow Wow Trail begins on what were once logging roads, then continues as a wilderness trail. It is a 29-mile loop.

Getting From the Entry Point to the Campsite

From the entry point, there is an easy 35-rod portage to the water. From there, we recommend one of the four campsites to the west and northwest of the entry point. We think the best campsite is located just 0.5 miles northwest from the entry point. It has large tent sites and is well protected from west and northwest winds.

Selecting a Campsite

If the site noted above is not available, you can paddle back to the south shore; there is another good site on the mainland about 1 mile to the west of the entry point. You will find another good mainland site less than 0.5 miles west again. If you want an island site, paddle just northeast for about 0.5 miles from that site. The site is on the south end of the island.

Entry Point 35-Isabella Lake

While You're There/Day Trip:

If you want, you can spend your whole visit exploring Isabella Lake, which requires no additional portaging after the initial portage. Isabella is one of the better entry-point walleye lakes and perch fishing here is also good. Work the white "gull rocks," the rocky points and rock piles throughout the lake.

DAY TRIP 1. We recommend a short canoe trip to the Island River. The trip starts at the west end of Isabella Lake with a 28-rod portage to the Isabella River, where you'll have a good chance to see moose, deer, beavers and eagles. There is a 20-rod portage before you turn left and head south on the Island River. You will encounter 2 more portages of approximately 3 rods and 13 rods along the river before you arrive at the entry point for the Island River. Here you can reverse your route and canoe back to Isabella Lake.

DAY TRIP 2. Those interested in hitting the trails can hike from the Isabella River, where the Pow Wow Trail crosses on a wooden foot bridge. Store your canoe here

Isabella entrance

and hike south to the trailhead at the Isabella Lake entry, where the lumber town of Forest Center once stood. Reverse the route and return to your canoe and then to your base camp on Isabella Lake, a round-trip of 2.5 miles.

DAY TRIP 3. You can also day-trip on the Isabella River to Rice Lake; this trip involves three portages of approximately 28 rods, 20 rods and 126 rods. Don't consider running the rapids, as they can be dangerous. Afterward, reverse the route from Rice Lake and return to your Isabella base camp.

PORTAGES TO GET TO CAMPSITE: 1, a 35-rod portage to Isabella Lake from the entry point

OPTIONAL PORTAGES (DAY TRIPS/HIKES): There are 4 portages on the Island River trip (28 rods, 20 rods, 3 rods, 13 rods); there are 3 portages to reach Rice Lake (28 rods, 20 rods, 126 rods)

DIFFICULTY: Easy

CAMPSITES: 10 on Isabella Lake

DAILY QUOTA: 3

SUGGESTED NUMBER OF DAYS: 3–5

Island vista

Entry Point 35-Isabella Lake

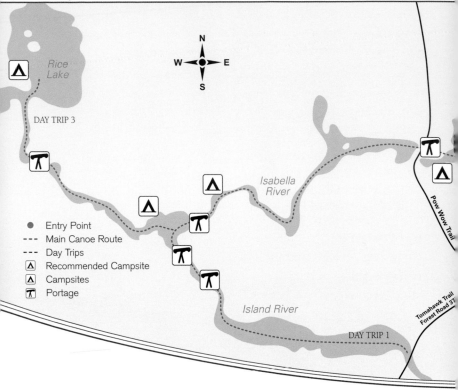

Rice Lake

DAY TRIP 3

Isabella River

- ● Entry Point
- --- Main Canoe Route
- --- Day Trips
- ⚠ Recommended Campsite
- ⚠ Campsites
- ⊼ Portage

Island River

DAY TRIP 1

Pow Wow Trail

Tomahawk Trail Forest Road 377

Directions to Entry Point:

From Silver Bay on MN-61, drive north for 5 miles and take a left onto MN-1. Drive on MN-1 for 20 miles. Just before you reach the town of Isabella, the road makes a sharp curve to the left; turn right here onto Forest Road 172. Take this for about 0.5 miles and turn left onto Forest Road 369. Drive for 10 miles until the road veers left, becoming Forest Road 373. After about 4 miles, turn right onto Forest Road 377 (the Tomahawk Trail). Take this about 4 miles to the entry point. The total driving distance is 41 miles.

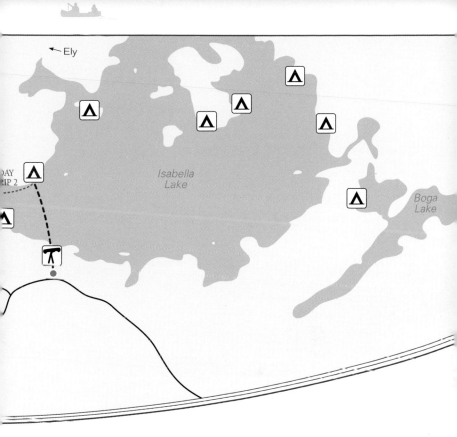

← Ely

Isabella
Lake

Boga
Lake

DAY
RIP 2

Things to Know Before You Go:

Maps: Fisher map 4; McKenzie map 19; Voyageur map 7
Longitude/Latitude: North 47° 48' 42"; West 91° 05' 6"
Contact/Outfitters: Ely, Tofte and Sawbill area outfitters
Lake Names: Isabella

Entry Point 36–Hog Creek

Hog Creek
portage starts

Why We Like This Trip

This is a relatively easy trip that features exceptional fishing and a trip down a winding wilderness stream where the shoreline sometimes encroaches on the water. At times, it almost feels like you are "bushwhacking" a new route to an unseen lake. This is a great choice for a family prepared for a long trip full of easy paddling (2 hours), which leads to a destination lake with good fishing and much to explore. Hog Creek is a narrow, meandering stream that empties into Perent Lake, a beautiful island-studded paradise with island campsites, great fishing and scenic vistas mostly unscathed by the Blowdown of 1999. A large lake,

- The leisurely paddle on Hog Creek to Perent Lake offers an excellent chance to see beavers, deer and moose.

- Perent Lake has many gorgeous islands, making an island campsite a great choice for this trip. The largest island on the northwest arm of the lake features spectacular views.

Perent is almost 1,600 acres, and features over 15 large islands and 20 campsites, most on the eastern side of the lake. Perent is a relatively shallow lake (its deepest point is 38 feet) and can be an outstanding walleye lake, even for beginners.

Getting From the Entry Point to the Campsite

The entry point features an easy stairway down to the creek. After you enter Hog Creek, turn left and there's a short paddle of about 5 minutes that leads to a rapids (the portage is on your right; this is the only portage on the trip). This is an easy, but fairly rocky, portage of only 10 rods. The portage is followed by 4 miles of paddling, which will take approximately 2 hours as you navigate the narrow stream through a series of tight bends and "S" curves as Hog Creek meanders toward Perent Lake. Settle into paddling and enjoy the trip in, but keep in mind that you may have to lift over some beaver dams, depending on the water level and beaver activity. On one of our trips here, we startled a beaver as we made one of the turns—he slapped his tail and was gone. We also startled several deer; the likelihood of a moose sighting is good. Be sure to watch the banks for signs of movement and tracks. And bring a

Entry Point 36–Hog Creek

good insect repellent, as this area can be buggy. Hog Creek eventually winds its way to Perent Lake, where we suggest taking the campsite on the northeast shore where Hog Creek enters the lake, if it is available. It is on the right as you enter the lake, and it has a good view and nice tent sites.

Selecting a Campsite

If you want an island site, you'll need to paddle about 2 miles to get to the best island campsites, two sites on opposite ends of the large island in the northeast section of the lake. These feature great views of the lake and the surrounding area. Note that the island campsites can be popular, so you may have to visit a few sites before finding your base camp.

While You're There/Day Trip:

Once you've established your base camp on the lake, why not go fishing? Perent Lake is a fishing destination and it is especially good for walleyes and

Hog Creek

northerns. Fish the islands, rocks and shoreline of this lake and your chances of catching walleyes are good.

Also, don't miss out on exploring the islands and the three large bays on the north end of the lake. The rocky outcrops here make for some dramatic scenery and there is often good berry picking in this area in July and August.

This large lake takes several days to truly explore, so most people will be satisfied with what it has to offer.

PORTAGES TO GET TO CAMPSITE: A 1- to 5-rod portage near the entry point on Hog Creek; you may have to lift over some beaver dams, depending on the water level and beaver activity

OPTIONAL PORTAGES (DAY TRIPS/HIKES): None

DIFFICULTY: Easy

CAMPSITES: 14 on the mainland and 6 island sites

DAILY QUOTA: 5

SUGGESTED NUMBER OF DAYS: 3–5

Hog Creek rock cliff

Entry Point 36-Hog Creek

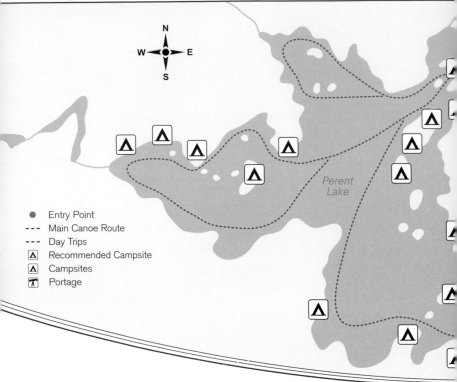

Legend:
- ● Entry Point
- --- Main Canoe Route
- --- Day Trips
- ⛺ Recommended Campsite
- ⛺ Campsites
- ⛵ Portage

Perent Lake

Directions to Entry Point:

These directions start in the town of Tofte. First drive north on MN-61 for about 1.5 miles and then turn left onto County Road 2, the Sawbill Trail. Drive on this road for about 15 miles, until you come to County Road 3. Turn left onto County Road 3 and drive about 5 miles until it becomes County Road 7. Take this for another 3 miles. Then turn right onto Forest Road 354 and drive about 1 mile until you see a sign for the Hog Creek Entry Point (#36) on your left. The total distance from Tofte is about 28 miles.

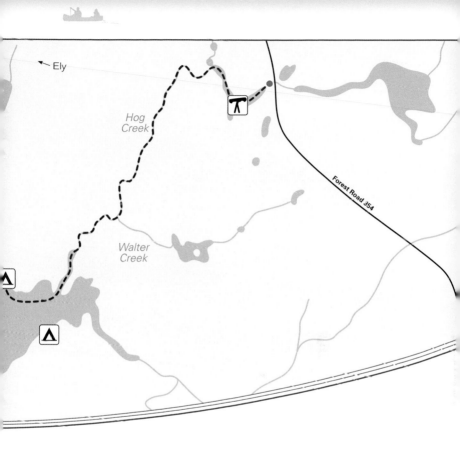

Ely

Hog
Creek

Walter
Creek

Forest Road 354

Things to Know Before You Go:

Maps: Fisher map 5; McKenzie map 20; Voyageur map 8
Longitude/Latitude: North 47° 48' 42"; West 91° 05' 6"
Contact/Outfitters: Ely, Tofte and Sawbill area outfitters
Lake Names: Perent

Entry Point 37–Kawishiwi Lake

Kawishiwi sandy beach

Why We Like This Trip

Kawishiwi Lake has some of the nicest sandy beach campsites in the BWCA, which should appeal to families and swimmers. It is a wonderful choice for first-time BWCA campers. It is a beautiful lake with many islands to explore and provides excellent photography opportunities and a chance to take pictures of a true wilderness lake. No portages are required to stay on Kawishiwi Lake. It also has some very good walleye fishing and provides the opportunity for some interesting day trips. Staying in the Kawishiwi National Forest Campground, just south of the lake, allows for a free overnight stay before you set off.

- Kawishiwi Lake is a drop-in lake, providing direct access to the BWCA. It is a great entry point for families.

- Kawishiwi Lake has numerous island campsites, and has many with sandy beaches, perfect for swimming or bathing.

Getting From the Entry Point to the Campsite

Kawishiwi is a drop-in lake and doesn't require an initial portage. From the entry point, a good campsite with a sandy beach is less than 0.25 miles to the right.

Selecting a Campsite

If the nearby campsite is taken, paddle about 0.75 miles to the northwest and locate one of the four nice campsites on the north side of the lake, or on the east side of a bay formed by a peninsula.

While You're There/Day Trip:

Spend the day relaxing, swimming and exploring the islands and bays of Kawishiwi Lake. The campsite that we recommend has a sandy beach, perfect for swimming. If children are in your group, make sure they wear their life vests when swimming. Kawishiwi Lake also has good walleye fishing, so spend some time fishing and exploring the lake.

DAY TRIP 1. Beginners will enjoy the trip from Kawishiwi Lake to Kawasachong Lake. Paddle to the narrow stream on the north end of Kawishiwi Lake and follow it to Square Lake. Most years you can paddle with no portages, but

Entry Point 37–Kawishiwi Lake

you may encounter beaver dams and possible lift-overs (lifting your canoe over a hazard). A stream flows out of the east side of Square Lake; follow it to another stream where you'll encounter portages of 20 rods and 11 rods as you canoe to Kawasachong Lake. From Kawasachong, you may want to hike the 189-rod portage on the north end to Townline Lake and reverse your route back to your base camp on Kawishiwi Lake.

DAY TRIP 2. Another option is the 69-rod portage from Square Lake to Baskatong Lake as a day hike.

Island of Kawishiwi

PORTAGES TO GET TO CAMPSITE: No portages to stay on Kawishiwi Lake

OPTIONAL PORTAGES (DAY TRIPS/HIKES): The day trip to Kawasachong Lake can require up to 2 portages, depending on water levels (20 rods, 12 rods); the hiking day trip from Square Lake to Baskatong Lake features a 69-rod hike, and the hike from Kawasachong Lake to Townline Lake is 189 rods

DIFFICULTY: Easy, no portages required for main trip

CAMPSITES: 7 sites on Kawishiwi, so get an early start and claim your site

DAILY QUOTA: 9

SUGGESTED NUMBER OF DAYS: 3–5

Kawishiwi sandy beach

Entry Point 37- Kawishiwi Lake

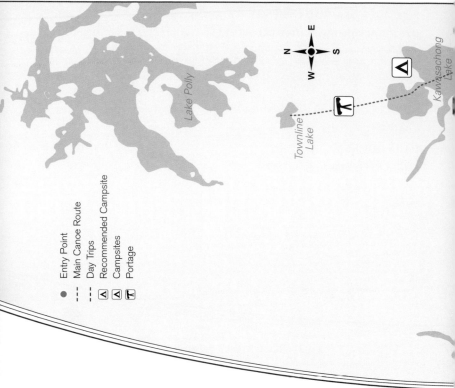

Directions to Entry Point:

These directions start in the town of Tofte. First drive north on MN-61 for about 1.5 miles and then turn left onto County Road 2, the Sawbill Trail. Drive on this road for about 15 miles until you come to County Road 3. Turn left onto County Road 3 and drive about 5 miles until it becomes County Road 7. Take this for another 3 miles. Then turn right onto Forest Road 354 and drive about 2 miles until you come to Entry Point #37. The total distance from Tofte is about 28 miles.

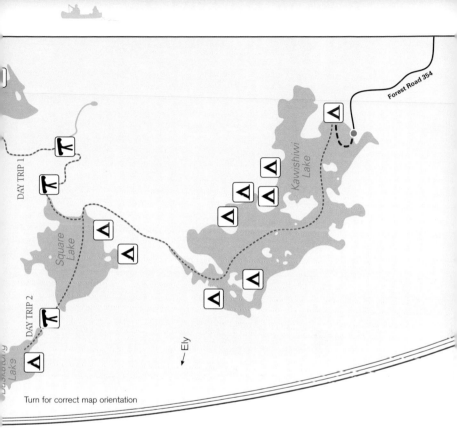

Forest Road 354

DAY TRIP 1

Kawishiwi Lake

Square Lake

DAY TRIP 2

Baskatong Lake

Ely

Turn for correct map orientation

Things to Know Before You Go:

Maps: Fisher map 5; McKenzie map 20; Voyageur map 8

Longitude/Latitude: North 47° 30' 21"; West 91° 06' 8"

Contact/Outfitters: Sawbill and Tofte area outfitters

Lake Names: Kawishiwi, Kawasachong, Townline, Square, Baskatong

Entry Point 38–Sawbill Lake

Camp entry point

Why We Like This Trip

Sawbill Lake is a great choice for the first-time BWCA camper. It is a drop-in lake and doesn't require an initial portage. In addition, the area is well traveled, as there is a National Forest campground next to the entry point, providing a place to stay overnight before entering the BWCA. It also has a small store where you can purchase things you might have forgotten to take along.

Sawbill Lake itself is a very long, relatively narrow lake running north and south. It is also a very clear lake with clarity of over 10 feet. Almost all of the lake is to the north of the entry point. Although there are 11 campsites, we recommend

- For those who want a BWCA experience, but don't want to stray far from civilization, head to Sawbill Lake. There is a Superior National Forest campground on the lake's southeast shore. This large campground has a store and outfitter and makes a good place to stay the night before you enter the BWCA.

- Sawbill Lake has some great hiking. In particular, the 460-rod portage between Lujenida and Zenith lakes makes a spectacular hike.

that you take the 30-rod portage into Alton Lake and base-camp there. The reason for this is that Alton has more of a wilderness feel and fewer people, yet you are just a short 30-rod portage from Sawbill, a store, and your vehicle. Like Sawbill, Alton is a clear, long, narrow lake, again running north and south, and it is also a good lake for smallmouth bass.

Getting From the Entry Point to the Campsite

To reach the base camp we recommend on Alton Lake, you first need to paddle from the Sawbill entry point to the opposite side of Sawbill Lake, about 0.75 miles to the northwest. Here you'll find the easy 30-rod portage. Once over the portage, head northwest for 0.75 miles; this will take you across the lake. There are two excellent campsites on the mainland, one just north of the other. Choose either of them if they are open.

Selecting a Campsite

If both of our recommended campsites are taken, there are two more good sites about 0.25 miles south, both on a small peninsula. If these are taken, continue south for 0.75 miles for another peninsular site.

Entry Point 38-Sawbill Lake

While You're There/Day Trip:

DAY TRIP 1. Paddle north from Alton Lake to the Kelso Lake portage. This 10-rod portage to Kelso Lake is easy, as it follows the bed of an old narrow gauge rail line, long gone. You will see wildflowers, including blue flag iris and water lilies in the bog area at the north end of Kelso. This bog area is a good place to look for moose, beaver and other wildlife. Photo opportunities abound.

DAY TRIP 2. The 460-rod portage at the north end of Lujenida Lake to Zenith Lake makes a good day-hike destination. (Most people would rather hike it than carry a canoe over it.)

DAY TRIP 3. A nice loop trip from Alton Lake involves taking the 10-rod portage to Kelso Lake. At the north end of the peninsula (shoreline) on your right, turn right and take the channel south to the 13-rod portage into Sawbill.

Sawbill fishing

Here you can paddle south on Sawbill to the Alton Lake portage and back to your campsite.

PORTAGES TO GET TO CAMPSITE: 1, a 30-rod portage from Sawbill Lake to Alton Lake

OPTIONAL PORTAGES (DAY TRIPS/HIKES): The portage from Alton Lake to Kelso Lake is 10 rods; the portage from Kelso to Sawbill is 13 rods; the day hike from Lujenida Lake to Zenith Lake is 460 rods

DIFFICULTY: Easy

CAMPSITES: 11 sites on Sawbill Lake, 16 sites on Alton Lake, 3 sites on Kelso Lake

DAILY QUOTA: 14

SUGGESTED NUMBER OF DAYS: 3–5

Sawbill campsite

Entry Point 38–Sawbill Lake

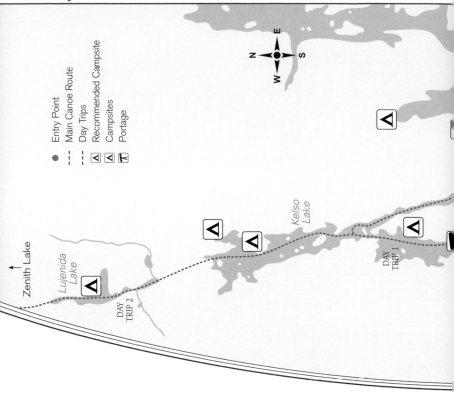

Directions to Entry Point:

From Tofte, drive north on MN-61 about 1.5 miles and then turn left onto County Road 2, the Sawbill Trail. Drive on this road for about 17 miles to the entry point, (#38). The total distance from Tofte to the entry point is 19 miles.

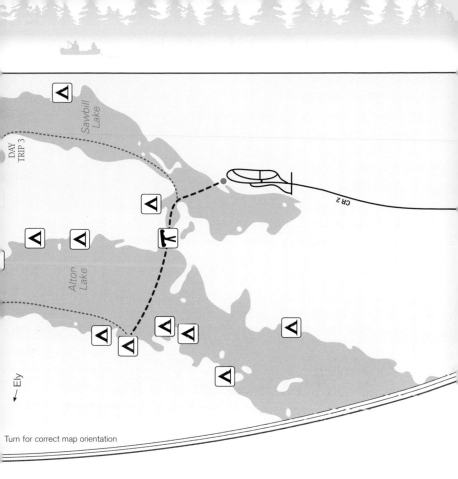

DAY TRIP 3

Sawbill Lake

Alton Lake

CR 2

← Ely

Turn for correct map orientation

Things to Know Before You Go:

 Maps: Fisher map 5; McKenzie map 21, Voyageur map 8
 Longitude/Latitude: North 47° 51' 49"; West 90° 53' 16"
 Contact/Outfitters: Ely, Tofte and Sawbill area outfitters
 Lake Names: Sawbill, Alton, Kelso, Lujenida, Zenith

Entry Point 39–Baker Lake

Baker Creek

Why We Like This Trip

The Baker Lake entry point includes a National Forest Service campground; Baker Lake Campground provides a place to stay free overnight before you enter. Baker Lake itself is very small and has a very intimate feeling to it. It does not, however, have any campsites located on it so you will need to take the 10-rod portage into Peterson Lake, another small lake that is long and narrow and not heavily used. It has one campsite. This means that you are likely to be the only party on it as you enjoy true solitude in the vast wilderness. Both Baker and Peterson are also shallow lakes, with good fishing for walleyes and northerns.

- A fairly remote entry point, Baker Lake leads to some small wilderness lakes that are easily accessible by short, easy portages.

- Along the shores of Baker and Peterson lakes you'll see evidence of the 1999 Blowdown and subsequent forest regeneration.

Getting From the Entry Point to the Campsite

Baker Lake is a drop-in lake and you don't need to portage to access it. Once on Baker Lake, head northwest for about 0.3 miles, until you come to the portage to Peterson Lake. This portage is 10 rods long; here you'll see evidence of the 1999 Blowdown. After the portage you will encounter a stream filled with boulders; on our last trip, we had to tow our canoe through these rocks. After this, keep the mainland on your right for 0.5 miles until you come to the campsite.

Selecting a Campsite

If our recommended campsite is taken, continue on with the mainland on your right for a mile (this takes about 25 minutes). This will take you to the boundary between Peterson Lake and Kelly Lake. Here there is a small set of rapids that you may need to wade through or portage around (3 rods). Afterward, you will come to three campsites inside a little bay on Kelly Lake.

Entry Point 39–Baker Lake

While You're There/Day Trip:

DAY TRIP 1. The 230-rod portage from Kelly Lake to Burnt Lake makes an interesting hiking trail and is fairly rugged, going up and down hills. We'd recommend hiking, not portaging, this route, as this would be a rugged portage for most beginners.

DAY TRIP 2. Day-trippers may enjoy paddling the narrow lakes and the Temperance River between Baker Lake and Weird Lake. Getting there requires three portages. The first portage (3 rods) occurs at the border between Peterson and Kelly Lake. It is followed by a 72-rod portage between Kelly Lake and Jack Lake; this portage is fairly level but can be slippery and muddy when wet. The final portage is 12 rods long from Jack Lake to Weird Lake and is fairly easy. Good photo opportunities abound throughout this route, with stands of wild rice and a variety of birds, including ducks and loons, as well as other wildlife.

Baker Lake portage end

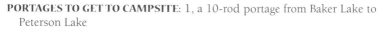

PORTAGES TO GET TO CAMPSITE: 1, a 10-rod portage from Baker Lake to Peterson Lake

OPTIONAL PORTAGES (DAY TRIPS/HIKES): The portage/day hike from Kelly Lake to Burnt Lake is 230 rods; the day trip on the Temperance River features three portages (3 rods, 72 rods, 12 rods)

DIFFICULTY: Easy

CAMPSITES: 1 on Peterson Lake, 4 on Kelly Lake and 1 on the Temperance River between Kelly Lake and Jack Lake

DAILY QUOTA: 3

SUGGESTED NUMBER OF DAYS: 3–5

Blowdown evidence

Entry Point 39–Baker Lake

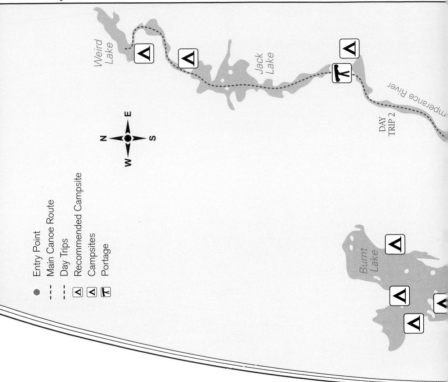

Directions to Entry Point:

From Tofte, drive on MN-61 north about 1.5 miles and then turn left onto County Road 2, the Sawbill Trail. Drive on this road for about 13 miles, until you come to Forest Road 165 (The Grade). Turn right and drive about 4 miles to Forest Road 1272. Turn left and drive about 0.5 miles to the entry point (#39). The total distance from Tofte to the entry point is about 20 miles.

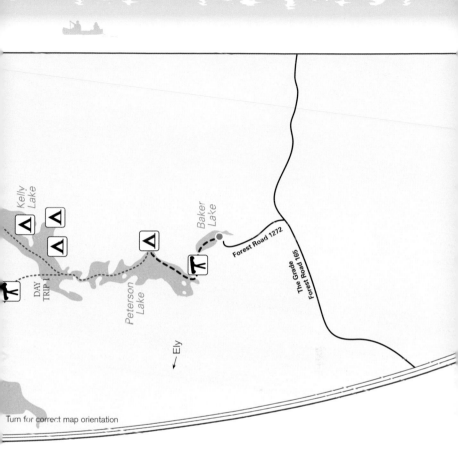

Turn for correct map orientation

Things to Know Before You Go:

Maps: Fisher map 6, McKenzie map 21, Voyageur map 8
Longitude/Latitude: North 47° 50' 42"; West 90° 49' 11"
Contact/Outfitters: Ely, Tofte and Sawbill area outfitters
Lake Names: Baker, Peterson, Kelly, Jack, Weird

Entry Point 40–Homer Lake

Portage to East Pipe

Why We Like This Trip

Homer Lake is a great entry point if you are looking for a small and remote lake that gives you a great wilderness experience. While motors are allowed on the eastern part of this lake, once you pass to the western part of the lake, only paddle power is allowed. There is good fishing in western Homer Lake, and many birds, including loons and eagles. You are close to portages to East Pipe Lake and Pipe Lake, which are off any of the standard canoe trip routes and are therefore very isolated. Here you will have a good chance to be alone in the wilderness.

HIGHLIGHTS

- A good entry choice for those who prefer a remote wilderness feel, Homer Lake features many secluded small lakes and streams.

- Homer Lake connects to Pipe Lake, a good place for a secluded respite, as it is only connected to one other lake by a portage.

Getting From the Entry Point to the Campsite

Homer is a drop-in lake at a boat launch. Paddle straight west for about 1 mile and you will see a sign designating the start of the BWCA. Continue paddling west another 1 mile, going south around a big island, and you will see a campsite just northwest on the western shore of Homer Lake. This makes a good base campsite.

Selecting a Campsite

If the campsite noted above is taken, paddle a little southeast and enter the narrow channel that will lead you to a 6-rod portage and then a 20-rod portage to East Pipe Lake. Turn right here and head west to the portages into Pipe Lake. The first is 5 rods long and the second is 3 rods long. Follow the northern shore for a little over 1 mile until you come to another good campsite. If this is also taken, round the point and head northwest to another good campsite.

Entry Point 40–Homer Lake

While You're There/Day Trip:

This area was subjected to fire in the 1990s and was affected by the 1999 Blow-down, so search open areas near Vern Lake for blueberries and evidence of new growth. Also, spend a day fishing for northern pike in the Pipe Lakes.

DAY TRIP 1. If you camp on Homer, you can take a trip of 6 rods to Whack Lake, though this portage is harder than the distance implies. This is followed by a portage of 14 rods from Whack Lake to Vern Lake. At Vern Lake, you can walk the portage to the western tip of Juno Lake (65 rods). This is a nice trip for seeing wildlife, especially eagles, and there is good fishing for northerns as well.

DAY TRIP 2. For a nice day trip, consider canoeing and portaging to East Pipe Lake or the Vern River.

Portage to Whack Lake

PORTAGES TO GET TO CAMPSITE: None on Homer Lake

OPTIONAL PORTAGES (DAY TRIPS/HIKES): From Homer Lake, 2 portages are required to reach East Pipe Lake (6 rods, 20 rods); 2 portages are required to reach Pipe Lake from East Pipe Lake (5 rods, 3 rods); the day trip to Whack Lake and Vern Lake requires 2 portages (6 rods, 14 rods) and the hike to Juno Lake is 65 rods

DIFFICULTY: Easy

CAMPSITES: 2 on Homer, 3 on Pipe Lake

DAILY QUOTA: 2

SUGGESTED NUMBER OF DAYS: 3–5

Homer campsite

Entry Point 40-Homer Lake

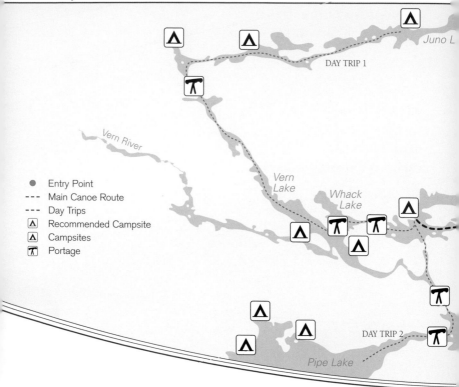

Directions to Entry Point:

These directions start in the town of Tofte. First drive north on MN-61 for about 1.5 miles and then turn left onto County Road 2, the Sawbill Trail. Drive on this road for about 13 miles to Forest Road 170. Turn right and drive about 11 miles to Forest Road 326. Turn left and drive 3 miles to the entry point (#40). The total distance from Tofte to the entry point is about 29 miles.

← Ely

Homer Lake

Brule Lake Road
Forest Road 326

East Pipe Lake

Things to Know Before You Go:

Maps: Fisher map 6; McKenzie map 21; Voyageur map 9

Longitude/Latitude: North 47° 54' 17"; West 90° 39' 36"

Contact/Outfitters: Ely, Tofte and Sawbill area outfitters

Lake Names: Homer, East Pipe, Pipe, Whack, Vern

Entry Point 41–Brule Lake

Juno portage

Why We Like This Trip

A trip on Brule can be spectacular. At almost 4,300 acres, Brule is one of the largest lakes in the BWCA, and it is very clear, with a water clarity of 15 feet. It has many large islands to explore, many with very good campsites. It is also a great fishing lake and features walleyes, northerns and smallmouth bass, and it provides access to Juno Lake, a smaller lake also noted for good fishing for walleyes and northerns.

However, be aware that as a large lake, Brule can become very rough and dangerous in windy conditions. The southern and eastern shores are safer in such

HIGHLIGHTS

- Brule is the largest lake in the BWCA where motors are completely banned.

- Fishing for northerns, walleyes and smallmouth on Brule is very good. Prior to the creation of the BWCA, Brule was a destination fishing lake with a popular fishing resort. The resort was removed when the lake became part of the BWCA.

conditions, but we recommend that only experienced paddlers attempt this lake. Brule is conveniently located near campgrounds in the Superior National Forest at Baker and Sawbill Lake; these are good choices for the night before you enter.

Getting From the Entry Point to the Campsite

You can drive your car to the entry point, unload your equipment, and then park your car in the lot about 100 yards away from the lake. After loading your canoe, you can shove off and head to your chosen campsite. We recommend going northeast from the entry point for about 200 yards until you come to a little point where the lake opens to the right. One of the best campsites on the lake is on this point, although it is very hard to see from the lake. If it is open, find a landing spot along the shore and climb up the rocks until you see the site nestled along a rock wall about 10 feet above the water and about 30 feet from the shore. This site has wonderful views of the lake in several directions and is very private because no one can see you from the lake. It also provides an excellent base camp for exploring the many islands in the area as well as the entire east end of Brule Lake.

Entry Point 41–Brule Lake

Selecting a Campsite

If the recommended site is unavailable, head northeast and travel toward a fairly large island just under 0.5 miles away. There is a good campsite on the southwest end of this island and another about 200 yards to the north. From the entry point, the Juno Lake portage is 2.4 miles to the east. To be closer to the Juno Lake portage (60 rods), keep the mainland on your left as you leave the entry point and paddle a little over 1.5 miles until you encounter a point jutting into the lake. A good campsite is nearby; it is well sheltered from the west and northwest winds of Brule.

While You're There/Day Trip:

DAY TRIP 1. We recommend a trip on the Juno portage to witness (and photograph) the evidence of the 1999 Blowdown. Seeing the damage up close (and nature regenerating) is amazing. This trip is possible from a base camp on Brule's south shore or from Juno Lake.

Hidden campsite

Also, consider taking a special hiking day trip after your stay on Brule or Juno. It requires a vehicle, but you can hike the Eagle Mountain Trail just north of Brule. This trailhead will take you to the highest point in Minnesota, with a spectacular view of the lakes and forest in the area. To get to Eagle Mountain from the Brule Lake parking lot, take Forest Road 326 south to Forest Road 170, turn left, and drive about 4 miles to the Eagle Mountain Trail. Turn left on this trail and drive to the trailhead, about 2.5 miles north.

PORTAGES TO GET TO CAMPSITE: None

OPTIONAL PORTAGES (DAY TRIPS/HIKES): To reach Juno Lake, there is a fairly easy portage of 60 rods

DIFFICULTY: Moderate, due to the likelihood of wind and waves on Brule Lake

CAMPSITES: 3 on Juno Lake and several on the more protected southern shore of Brule

DAILY QUOTA: 10

SUGGESTED NUMBER OF DAYS: 5

Brule campsite

Entry Point 41-Brule Lake

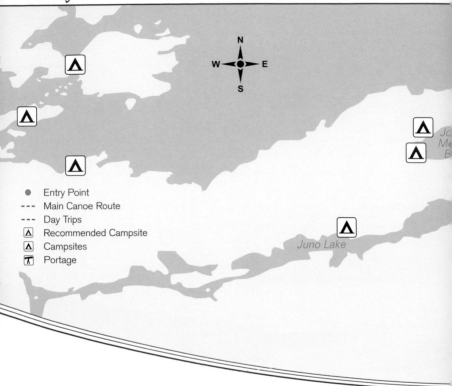

Entry Point
- - - Main Canoe Route
- - - Day Trips
- Recommended Campsite
- Campsites
- Portage

Juno Lake

Directions to Entry Point:

These directions start in the town of Tofte. Drive north on MN-61 for about 1.5 miles and then turn left onto County Road 2, the Sawbill Trail. Drive on this road for about 13 miles to Forest Road 170. Turn right and drive about 11 miles to Forest Road 326. Turn left and drive 5 miles to the entry point (#41). The total distance from Tofte to the entry point is about 31 miles.

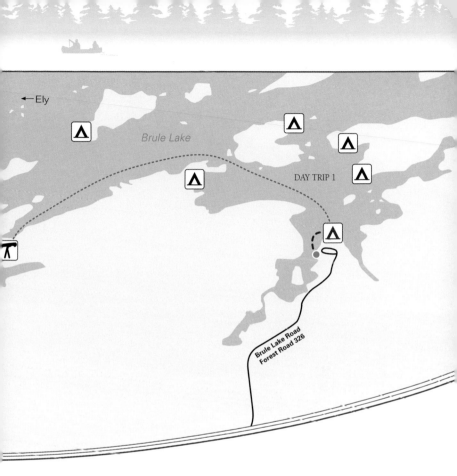

← Ely

Brule Lake

DAY TRIP 1

Brule Lake Road
Forest Road 326

Things to Know Before You Go:

    Maps: Fisher maps 6 and 12; McKenzie map 21; Voyageur map 9

    Longitude/Latitude: North 47° 48′ 34″, West 90° 38′ 41″

    Contact/Outfitters: Ely, Tofte and Sawbill area outfitters

    Lake Names: Brule, Juno

East Area Trips

East Area Trips

Grand Marais, located on the shore of Lake Superior, is an art-centered community with numerous galleries, restaurants, and a school devoted to teaching many types of folk art. It serves as the southern gateway to the famous Gunflint Trail (County Road 12) and the Arrowhead Trail (County Road 16) near Hovland. These trails serve as entry points to the eastern portion of the BWCA.

Table of Contents

Missing Link Lake - Entry Point 51. 134

Sea Gull Lake - Entry Point 54 140

Duncan Lake - Entry Point 60. 146

Clearwater Lake - Entry Point 62 152

East Bearskin Lake - Entry Point 64 158

John Lake - Entry Point 69 164

Entry Point 51–Missing Link Lake

Tuscarora portage

Why We Like This Trip

Missing Link Lake is a small lake in a very private setting, and it is a great wilderness escape. It is also a designated brook trout lake (you need a trout stamp on your fishing license to fish there), and it's no surprise that it's very good for brook trout; two thousand fingerlings are stocked in Missing Link Lake every year. This lake also has some interesting day trip opportunities, including hiking the rugged 428-rod Tuscarora portage, and the lake also provides many opportunities for photography, as the rocky shores and tall stands of timber are picturesque, and there is abundant wildlife.

- Missing Link is a small, intimate lake to explore. All the campsites are on rocky outcrops. Missing Link is also a designated brook trout lake. (You need a trout endorsement or stamp on your license to fish on it.)

- Missing Link provides access to the famous Tuscorara Portage, a hike of over a mile that many consider to be one of the toughest portages in the whole BWCA. It features some excellent vistas.

Getting From the Entry Point to the Campsite

The Missing Link entry point is accessed on Round Lake. You drop your canoe into Round Lake and then paddle to the southwest corner of the lake until you come to the Missing Link portage, which is 138 rods long. This is a rocky portage, with poor footing, and is fairly challenging when you are carrying a full load. From the end of the portage, we recommend the campsite less than 0.25 miles to the left.

Selecting a Campsite

If our recommended campsite is taken, head south along the western shoreline for about 0.3 miles to find another nice site. The last site on this lake is about 0.25 miles south of this one.

While You're There/Day Trip:

You should consider spending a day fishing on Missing Link for its brook trout. We bring crawlers and leeches, but many fishermen prefer fly-fishing or artificial lures with a spinning rod. All can be effective, but do your part to conserve the resource and keep only enough trout for a meal.

Entry Point 51-Missing Link Lake

DAY TRIP 1. From your base camp on Missing Link, you can hike the famous (or infamous) Tuscarora portage between Missing Link and Tuscarora Lake (428 rods). It is a long, rugged and interesting portage that climbs throughout and then drops steeply to Tuscarora Lake. Many consider it to be one of the most difficult portages in the BWCA. It is even more difficult to climb out of Tuscarora Lake and return to Missing Link Lake. It is a very difficult portage if you carry a canoe and gear over it. Beginners should hike it and enjoy the views along the way, as photo opportunities abound. Bring a camera and walk quietly and you might come across some wildlife. Sit, rest and watch when you need to. You can expect to see others, as it is a popular entry to the more remote parts of the BWCA. You'll see Tuscarora Lake and you can then return to your base camp on Missing Link.

DAY TRIP 2. The portage from Missing Link Lake to Snipe Lake is another hiking opportunity from your base camp. A 180-rod portage, it is slightly longer than

Portage to Missing Lake from Round Lake

the portage from Round Lake to Missing Link Lake, but it seems easier and flatter. Bring your camera, sit and listen on the portage and enjoy the hike. Ambitious day-trippers may bring a canoe over the portage to fish and explore on Snipe Lake before returning to their base camp on Missing Link.

PORTAGES TO GET TO CAMPSITE: 1, Round Lake to Missing Link, 138 rods

OPTIONAL PORTAGES (DAY TRIPS/HIKES): The hike from Missing Link to Tuscarora Lake is 428 rods; the portage/hike from Missing Link to Snipe is 180 rods

DIFFICULTY: Moderate

CAMPSITES: 3 on Missing Link Lake

DAILY QUOTA: 5

SUGGESTED NUMBER OF DAYS: 3–5

Meadow on Tuscarora portage

Entry Point 51-Missing Link Lake

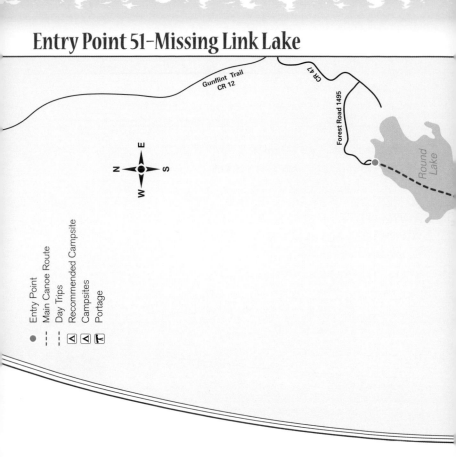

Directions to Entry Point:

The Missing Link–Round Lake entry point is located about 43 miles north of Grand Marais. At the north end of Grand Marais, turn off MN-61 onto County 12, the Gunflint Trail. After 42 miles, turn left on County 47. After about 0.25 miles, look for Forest Road 1495 and turn right and drive to the Missing Link entry point (#51) on Round Lake.

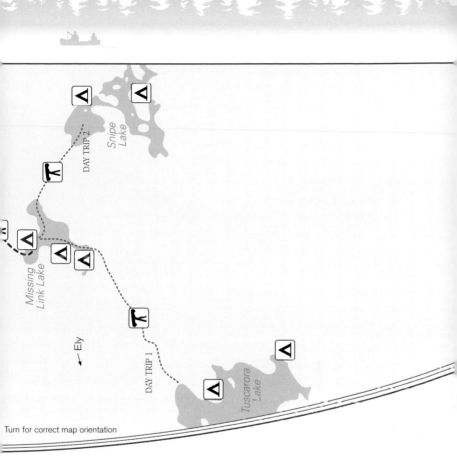

Turn for correct map orientation

Things to Know Before You Go:

Maps: Fisher map 5; McKenzie map 7; Voyageur map 6
Longitude/Latitude: West 48° 04' 28"; West 90° 50' 14"
Contact/Outfitters: Gunflint Trail area outfitters
Lake Names: Round, Missing Link, Snipe, Tuscarora

Entry Point 54–Sea Gull Lake

Channel near Sea Gull Lake

Why We Like This Trip

Sea Gull Lake is famous for its palisades, gigantic rock cliffs that rise right out of the lake. About 4,000 acres in size, Sea Gull Lake is large, and it is very clear as well, with a clarity of about 14 feet. A drop-in lake, Sea Gull requires no initial portage. There are two public landings on Sea Gull, the Trails End Campground on the northern end of the lake, and the Blankenburg public landing. The GPS coordinates we're listing are from the Blankenburg landing.

The lake has many islands and channels to explore and also has many very nice campsites. Be aware, however, that the eastern part of this lake is not in the

HIGHLIGHTS

- Sea Gull Lake is a beautiful, large lake with many islands and it is perfect for those who would rather paddle than portage. You can put in at Sea Gull and spend your entire time on this huge lake.

- Sea Gull has some tremendous palisades, huge rocky cliffs rising right out of the water. Blueberry picking is exceptional in the open areas near the lake that were impacted by fires, controlled burns and the 1999 Blowdown.

BWCA and motorized boats are allowed. If you head in a northwestern direction for about 2 miles, you will enter the BWCA and see no more motorboats.

Getting From the Entry Point to the Campsite

The campsite we recommend is located near the Sea Gull Lake palisades, and is large and open. Getting there, however, can be a challenge. Because Sea Gull is a large and complicated lake, we strongly urge you to get a Fisher E8 map from an outfitter before you set out. From the Blankenburg entry point, paddle west until you encounter Fishhook Island. Continue paddling west, and keep the northern tip of Fishhook Island on your left and the mainland on your right. After about 0.75 miles, you will come to Trails End Channel, which opens to the north. Continue west for another 0.5 miles, keeping the mainland on your right until the land begins to head north. At this point, you'll see several islands ahead of you; toward the northern end of these islands there is a narrow passage between two of them. Pass through this and you should see a sign indicating the start of the BWCA. After passing through the channel, turn southwest, keeping the mainland some distance off to your right. You will then pass by several islands; a little over 0.5 miles from the passage, the lake narrows and

Entry Point 54-Sea Gull Lake

the palisades begin. Follow the palisades around the peninsula and then head northwest, keeping the mainland on your right. You will soon see a large, flat rock leading down to the water. This is where the campsite is located.

Selecting a Campsite

If our recommended campsite is taken, select any site along the north shore or the one on an island just south of our recommended site. If you paddle back around the palisades, keeping them on your left and a large island on your right, a nice campsite is to the east after the lake opens in that direction. Again, be sure to consult a good map. We generally recommend that people stay in the northern and western parts of Sea Gull, as the other areas were severely damaged in the 1999 Blowdown and by three later forest fires.

While You're There/Day Trip:

Plan to camp near the palisades and explore the area. It is easier to navigate with a good map and by using the shoreline to your north as a reference point.

Sea Gull Lake rock cliff

DAY TRIP 1. As a day trip, go to Gull Lake. To get there, follow the map toward Trails End Channel. Take the channel on your left and then the 38-rod portage. Heading north through some small bays, you will then enter Gull Lake.

DAY TRIP 2. On Sea Gull Lake, you can choose to hire an outfitter to tow you through the southern part of nearby Saganaga Lake to Red Rock Bay, where you can take the short portage (9 rods) into Red Rock Lake, with its good fishing and natural beauty. You can also arrange a reverse tow and a pick-up time. Without a tow, this trip would require far too much paddling and portaging for a day trip for beginners.

PORTAGES TO GET TO CAMPSITE: None, if you stay on Sea Gull Lake

OPTIONAL PORTAGES (DAY TRIPS/HIKES): There is a 38-rod portage on the trip to Gull Lake; there is a 9-rod portage from Saganaga to Red Rock Lake

DIFFICULTY: Easy in calm water; moderate if the wind is blowing

CAMPSITES: 40 on Sea Gull Lake

DAILY QUOTA: 13

SUGGESTED NUMBER OF DAYS: 4

Campsite on Sea Gull Lake

Entry Point 54–Sea Gull Lake

- ● Entry Point
- --- Main Canoe Route
- --- Day Trips
- ◬ Recommended Campsite
- ◬ Campsites
- ⊼ Portage

N
W ◆ E
S

Saganaga Lake

Alpine Lake

Sea Gull Lake

Ely

Directions to Entry Point:

The Sea Gull Lake entry point is located 50 miles north of Grand Marais. At the north end of Grand Marais, turn off MN-61 onto County 12, the Gunflint Trail. Stay on this road until you see the Blankenburg entry point to Sea Gull Lake (#54). Turn left into the parking lot at this landing.

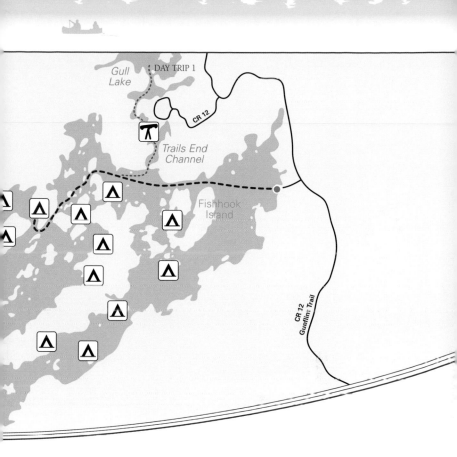

Things to Know Before You Go:

Maps: Fisher maps F8 and 19, 32; McKenzie map 6 and 7; Voyageur map 6

Longitude/Latitude: North 48° 08' 50"; West 90° 52' 10"

Contact/Outfitters: Gunflint Trail area outfitters

Lake Names: Sea Gull, Gull, Saganaga, Red Rock

Entry Point 60–Duncan Lake

Waterfall between
Duncan and Rose lakes

Why We Like This Trip

Duncan Lake is a relatively small, but lovely, lake and a great place to base-camp.
Its most famous feature is the Stairway Portage (90 rods) on the lake's north end.
As its name implies, the portage has a stairway of about 90 steps. This portage
also has a spectacular waterfall. The steps take you to Rose Lake, part of the US-
Canada border. As a border lake, it is also part of the route the Voyageurs of old
took to reach far into the interior of the continent.

In addition to historical attractions, Duncan Lake has some nice campsites and
there are some great day trips nearby.

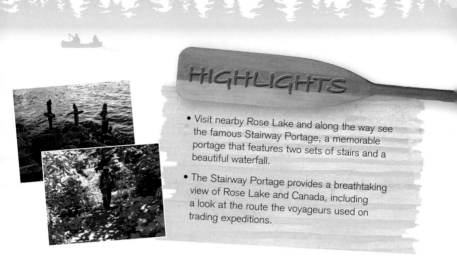

- Visit nearby Rose Lake and along the way see the famous Stairway Portage, a memorable portage that features two sets of stairs and a beautiful waterfall.

- The Stairway Portage provides a breathtaking view of Rose Lake and Canada, including a look at the route the voyageurs used on trading expeditions.

Getting From the Entry Point to the Campsite

To reach Duncan Lake from entry point #60, two short portages are required. Don't let these portages worry you, as they are both easy. At the entry point, there is a short portage of 7 rods to Bearskin Lake. Once on Bearskin Lake, paddle to the northwest corner where there is a bay; the easy 77-rod portage to Duncan Lake is located here. Once you have entered Duncan, we recommend the campsite that is less than 0.25 miles to the west (left) of the end of the portage.

Selecting a Campsite

If the recommended campsite is occupied, paddle northwest and you will find a nice site at the end of a peninsula. If this is taken, continue northwest, passing a long, narrow bay until you come to the western shore of the lake. There is a campsite just north of the bay and three more along this western shore.

While You're There/Day Trip:

DAY TRIP 1. The highlight of this trip is a visit to Rose Lake over the Stairway Portage. Plan to hike the 90-rod stairway portage. It includes a good climb

Entry Point 60–Duncan Lake

up two series of steps and a beautiful waterfall. When you arrive at Rose Lake you can look across to the Canadian shore, so be sure to bring your camera.

DAY TRIP 2. If you hike the Rose Lake Stairway Portage, you will cross both the Border Route Trail and the Caribou Rock Trail, giving you additional hiking options.

DAY TRIP 3. If you would like a nice, rugged day hike, you can also hike the portage from Duncan to Partridge Lake (173 rods), from the bay on the southwest shore of Duncan Lake. Whichever hiking option you choose, consult a good map and bring a daypack with food, water, matches, a poncho and a compass.

Portage from Duncan Lake
to Bearskin Lake

PORTAGES TO GET TO CAMPSITE: 2, one of 7 rods from the parking lot to Bearskin Lake, and one of 77 rods from Bearskin to Duncan Lake

OPTIONAL PORTAGES (DAY TRIPS/HIKES): The trip to Rose Lake and the Stairway Portage is 90 rods; the day hike from Duncan Lake to Partridge Lake is 173 rods

DIFFICULTY: Easy to moderate

CAMPSITES: 7

DAILY QUOTA: 4

SUGGESTED NUMBER OF DAYS: 4

Portage between Duncan Lake and Bearskin Lake

Entry Point 60–Duncan Lake

Directions to Entry Point:

The Duncan Lake entry point is located about 26 miles north of Grand Marais. At the northern end of Grand Marais, turn off MN-61 onto County 12, also known as the Gunflint Trail. After about 28 miles, turn right onto County Road 65. Follow this road for about 2 miles until you see the sign for Bearskin Lake and turn left into the parking lot.

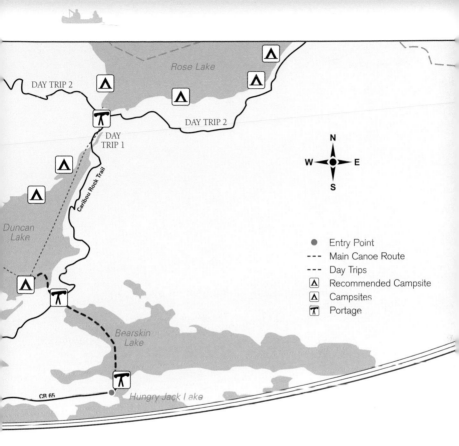

Things to Know Before You Go:

Maps: Fisher map 13; McKenzie map 2; Voyageur map 9

Longitude/Latitude: North 48° 03' 44"; West 90° 26' 39"

Contact/Outfitters: Gunflint Trail area outfitters

Lake Names: Bearskin, Duncan, Rose, Partridge

Entry Point 62–Clearwater Lake

Border Route Trail crossing
on Mountain Lake portage

Why We Like This Trip

Clearwater Lake is well named, as it boasts a water clarity of 25 feet. Clearwater is located just off the Gunflint Trail and is a beautiful, interesting lake and requires no portages to other lakes. The south shore of Clearwater has a spectacular rocky cliff area known as the Clearwater Palisades. These are located well above the waterline and are very impressive and photogenic. Clearwater also has some very good campsites, with excellent vistas of the palisades.

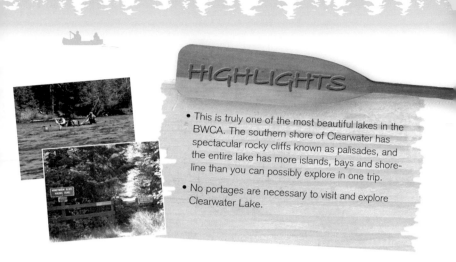

HIGHLIGHTS

- This is truly one of the most beautiful lakes in the BWCA. The southern shore of Clearwater has spectacular rocky cliffs known as palisades, and the entire lake has more islands, bays and shoreline than you can possibly explore in one trip.

- No portages are necessary to visit and explore Clearwater Lake.

Getting From the Entry Point to the Campsite

Clearwater Lake is a drop-in lake that doesn't require an initial portage. The entry point has a small parking lot and a boat launch; boats with motors of up to 10 horsepower are allowed throughout Clearwater Lake. The boat launch is located on the north side of the lake, as are all the campsites. We recommend that you keep the mainland on your left side for about 1.25 miles, until you reach a campsite. We recommend you take this excellent campsite, as it has excellent tent sites and great views of the palisades on the south shore.

Selecting a Campsite

If the first campsite is occupied, the next three along the north shore are also good options, but note that farther up the shore, the views of the palisades are less impressive.

While You're There/Day Trip:

From your base camp, paddling and hiking near the palisades and cliffs on the southeast shore of Clearwater Lake make for a nice day trip. Spend a day fishing the clear depths of Clearwater for lake trout. Try shallow water early in

Entry Point 62–Clearwater Lake

the season and deeper water as the season progresses. A portable depth finder is helpful here. Smallmouth bass are also plentiful in Clearwater Lake.

DAY TRIP 1. If you want to go further afield, visit historic Mountain Lake, a border lake with nice views of Canada. To get there, paddle to the northeast part of the lake, about 4 miles from the entry point, and hike the fairly easy 90-rod portage. The famous Border Route Trail crosses the Mountain Lake Portage, and while you're hiking the portage to Mountain Lake, you may want to take a short hike on the Border Route Trail.

DAY TRIP 2. For a more difficult hike, attempt the 200-rod portage to Caribou Lake. The portage is located on the southeast side of Clearwater, and it climbs sharply and is fairly rocky with poor footing. (It is more enjoyable as a hike than as a portage.)

Clearwater Palisades

When you finish your stay on Clearwater Lake, leave time to hike the Honeymoon Bluff Trail off of Clearwater Road (County Road 66) near the Flour Lake Campground. The trailhead is on your right as you're leaving Clearwater Lake. It has spectacular views of several lakes and is approximately a 0.5-mile loop. The trail is fairly steep and we wouldn't recommend it for children as there are some areas with drop-offs.

PORTAGES TO GET TO CAMPSITE: None

OPTIONAL PORTAGES (DAY TRIPS/HIKES): The portage to Mountain Lake is 90 rods; the day hike/portage to Caribou Lake is 200 rods

DIFFICULTY: Easy

CAMPSITES: 6

DAILY QUOTA: 4

SUGGESTED NUMBER OF DAYS: 3

Clearwater Palisades

Entry Point 62–Clearwater Lake

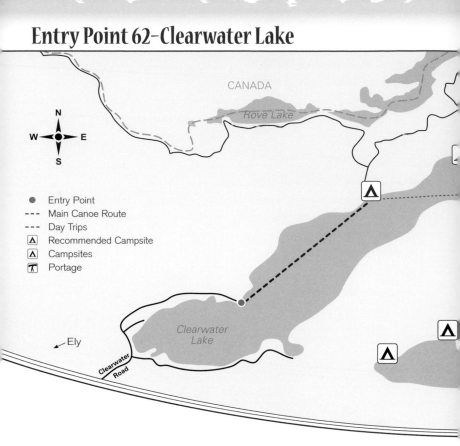

Directions to Entry Point:

The Clearwater entry point is located about 31 miles north of Grand Marais. At the north end of Grand Marais, turn off MN-61 onto County 12, the Gunflint Trail. Take this for about 27 miles to Clearwater Road (County Road 66) and turn right, and take this 4 miles to the entry point, which is a public boat landing.

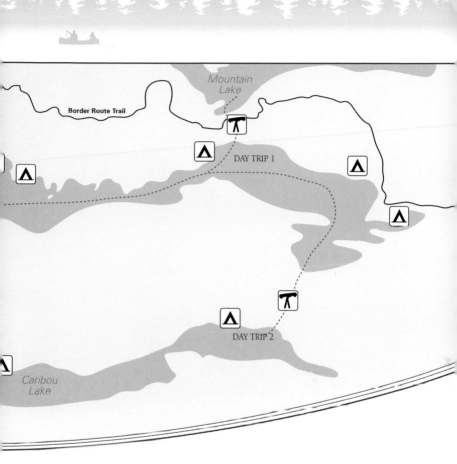

Mountain
Lake

Border Route Trail

DAY TRIP 1

DAY TRIP 2

Caribou
Lake

Things to Know Before You Go:

Maps: Fisher maps 13 and 14; McKenzie map 2; Voyageur map 10

Longitude/Latitude: North 48° 04' 31"; West 90° 22' 06"

Contact/Outfitters: Gunflint Trail area outfitters

Lake Names: Clearwater, Mountain, Caribou

Entry Point 64-East Bearskin Lake

Alder Lake vista

Why We Like This Trip

East Bearskin Lake is a long, narrow lake that runs from southwest to northeast, and takes the shape of a "Y" at its eastern end. Because it is so narrow, you are always close to land. It gives you the feeling of being in the center of a heavily timbered wilderness. Be aware that motors can be used throughout East Bearskin Lake. There is a Superior National Forest campground (East Bearskin Campground) where you can stay the night before you enter and you can launch from there. Our GPS coordinates are from this landing. While there are only two campsites on East Bearskin Lake, a 48-rod portage takes you into attractive and

HIGHLIGHTS

- From East Bearskin, take the hike to Johnson Falls, one of the most spectacular falls in the BWCA. Johnson Falls is actually three beautiful, closely grouped falls. They are worth the trip.

- Nearby Alder Lake is a scenic lake with cliffs and palisades on its southern shore as well as impressive pines on the shoreline (and in some campsites).

charming Alder Lake, which has cliffs and palisades on its south shore. Alder Lake has 10 sites, and it provides access to several lakes, including Canoe Lake, where you can hike the 232-rod portage to Pine Lake and see the lovely Johnson Falls.

Getting From the Entry Point to the Campsite

You can launch your canoe from East Bearskin Campground without a portage; however, a portage is required to get the campsite we recommend on Alder Lake. From the landing, first paddle northeast for about 0.25 miles. Now keep the south shore of the mainland on your right for about 1.5 miles. Here East Bearskin forms a "Y." Keep to the south shore (the right part of the "Y") for a little over 1 mile and when the lake narrows, begin looking for the 48-rod portage to Alder Lake on the north (left) shore. Cross this portage and then paddle northeast for about 0.75 miles. You will then come to a nice campsite on the north shore (on your left).

Selecting a Campsite

If our recommended campsite is taken, continue on for another mile and there are three nice campsites on the north (left) shore of Alder Lake.

Entry Point 64-East Bearskin Lake

While You're There/Day Trip:

Plan on spending a couple of days fishing for walleye, smallmouth and lake trout on East Bearskin and Alder Lake.

DAY TRIP 1. You can portage to a number of different lakes from Alder Lake. From your Alder base camp, take the 22-rod portage to Canoe Lake and spend some time there fishing and exploring.

DAY TRIP 2. For another nice day trip take the 19-rod portage from Alder to Pierz Lake and explore. Pierz's three campsites make a great stop for a lunch break.

DAY TRIP 3. If you want to hike, visit Johnson Falls. To get there, take the 22-rod portage to Canoe Lake and leave your canoe in the woods at the start of the 232-rod portage to Pine Lake. Hike the portage to Pine Lake; at the end of the portage a trail will take you to Johnson Falls. Be sure to bring a daypack.

Palisades on Alder Lake

DAY TRIP 4. If you want to canoe on several lakes, you can take a canoe day trip that loops from Alder Lake into two sections of East Bearskin Lake and back into Alder. From your base camp on Alder, go northeast for less than 0.25 miles and take the 80-rod portage into the northeast arm of East Bearskin Lake. Then paddle southwest, keeping the mainland on your left, around the point and back to the Alder Lake portage in the southeast arm of East Bearskin. The 48-rod portage will take you back to Alder and your base camp.

PORTAGES TO GET TO CAMPSITE: 1, from the southeast arm of East Bearskin to Alder, 48 rods

OPTIONAL PORTAGES (DAY TRIPS/HIKES): The trip from Alder Lake to Canoe Lake has a 22-rod portage; the portage from Alder to Pierz is 22 rods; the trip to Johnson Falls has a 22-rod portage, followed by a 232-rod hike; the loop trip has two portages (80 rods, 48 rods)

DIFFICULTY: Easy

CAMPSITES: 2 on East Bearskin and 7 on Alder Lake

DAILY QUOTA: 5

SUGGESTED NUMBER OF DAYS: 5

Canoe Lake vista

Entry Point 64–East Bearskin Lake

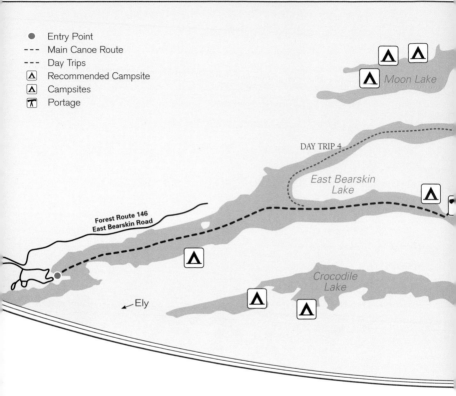

Legend:
- ● Entry Point
- – – – Main Canoe Route
- – – – Day Trips
- ⛺ Recommended Campsite
- ⛺ Campsites
- ⛓ Portage

Moon Lake

DAY TRIP 4

East Bearskin Lake

Forest Route 146
East Bearskin Road

Crocodile Lake

← Ely

Directions to Entry Point:

The East Bearskin Lake entry point is located about 23 miles north of Grand Marais. At the north end of Grand Marais, turn off MN-61 onto County 12 (the Gunflint Trail). After about 25 miles you will pass Bear Cub Lake. Take a right on the next road, Forest Road 146 (East Bearskin Road), and drive for about 1.5 miles to the East Bearskin Campground and entry point.

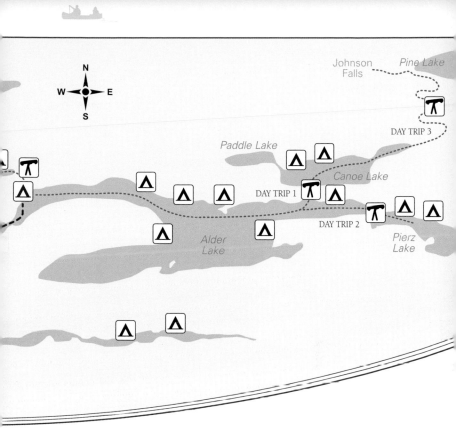

Things to Know Before You Go:

Maps: Fisher map 14; McKenzie map 2, Voyageur map 10

Longitude/Latitude: North 48° 22' 12"; West 90° 23' 25"

Contact/Outfitters: Gunflint Trail area outfitters

Lake Names: East Bearskin, Alder, Pine, Canoe, Pierz

Entry Point 69–John Lake

Portage to creek
toward Fowl Lake

Why We Like This Trip

John Lake is our favorite BWCA lake. This is the place to go if you want to feel alone in the vast wilderness. It is a beautiful lake that is located off the beaten path, and because it has a daily quota of only 1, it gets much less traffic than the Gunflint Trail lakes. With such a small quota, you need to apply early to get a permit. It is a small lake of only about 190 acres, but it is surrounded by high, densely wooded hills. John Lake also features some interesting day trips, and we always have very good luck fishing for walleyes and northerns here, as the lake is shallow, never over 20 feet deep.

HIGHLIGHTS

- This is a very remote entry and a wonderful area for the beginning BWCA camper. You will see high hills covered with a mix of birch and conifers, with trees right down to the water's edge.

- You can spend the entire trip on narrow, beautiful and peaceful John Lake. You can also explore the Royal River and South Fowl Lake where you can see the historic route the voyageurs used to take.

Getting From the Entry Point to the Campsite

To get to John Lake, begin by launching your canoe at the boat landing and dock on Little John Lake, then paddle about 0.5 miles to the short and shallow rapids into John Lake. We have always been able to run these rapids, but if you'd rather not, there is a 10-rod portage on the left side. The campsite we recommend is 0.25 miles across the lake on the northeast shore by the entrance to the Royal River. It is slightly elevated and has great views.

Selecting a Campsite

If the campsite we recommend is taken, there is a nice campsite on the right, near where you entered John Lake from Little John Lake. There is also a nice campsite on the north shore of John Lake, under 0.5 miles from the entrance to Little John.

While You're There/Day Trip:

DAY TRIP 1. You can have a nice day trip exploring the 207-rod portage to beautiful East Pike Lake. You may find berries and you'll see some evidence of the 1999 Blowdown. The fishing is good too; we have caught smallmouth bass right at the end of the portage from shore. Ambitious anglers will be well rewarded if they carry a canoe and fish a day on East Pike Lake. We always day-trip to East Pike to fish.

DAY TRIP 2. You can take the 61-rod portage in the southeast corner of John Lake to the narrow Royal River which widens into small, weedy Royal Lake. From there, you can hike the fairly rough 96-rod portage to see the entrance to historic South Fowl Lake, which was an early voyageur route on the Canadian border.

John Lake campsite

PORTAGES TO GET TO CAMPSITE: 1, from Little John Lake to John Lake, 10 rods

OPTIONAL PORTAGES (DAY TRIPS/HIKES): The trip from John Lake to East Pike Lake has 1 portage (207 rods); the trip from John Lake to Royal Lake/South Fowl Lake has 2 portages (61 rods, 96 rods)

DIFFICULTY: Easy

CAMPSITES: 3 on John Lake

DAILY QUOTA: 1

SUGGESTED NUMBER OF DAYS: 3 or 4

John Lake portage

Entry Point 69–John Lake

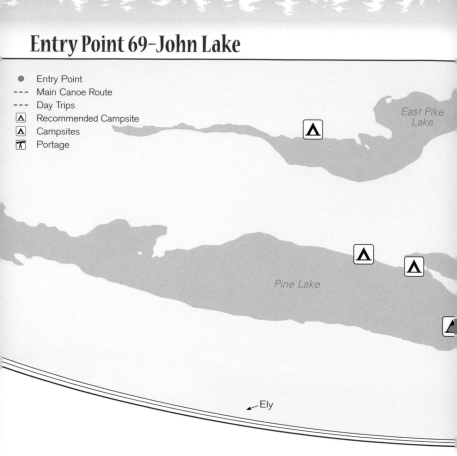

- ● Entry Point
- --- Main Canoe Route
- --- Day Trips
- Ⓐ Recommended Campsite
- Ⓐ Campsites
- Ⓣ Portage

East Pike Lake

Pine Lake

←Ely

Directions to Entry Point:

From Grand Marais, take MN-61 north 19 miles to Hovland. Here, turn left onto County Road 16, the Arrowhead Trail. Take this for about 17 miles until you come to a "Y" intersection (about 2 miles past Otter Lake). Bear to the right here. Then drive about 2 miles, passing McFarland Lake, and continue to the entry point on Little John Lake. The total distance from Grand Marais to John Lake is 38 miles.

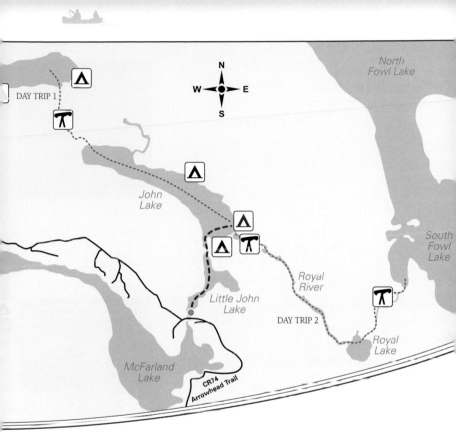

Things to Know Before You Go:

  Maps: Fisher map 14; McKenzie map 1; Voyageur map 10
  Longitude/Latitude: North 48° 03' 16"; West 90° 03' 25"
  Contact/Outfitters: Grand Marais and Gunflint Trail area outfitters
  Lake Names: Little John, John, East Pike, Royal, South Fowl

About the Authors

Van Jordahl is a Minnesota native with a Masters of Science degree from Bemidji State University and a Sixth Year degree from Mankato State University, both in Educational Administration. He is a retired Minnesota elementary school principal. He has had a lifetime love of fishing and exploring the BWCA and the Superior National Forest. He has planned and guided trips to the BWCA for youth groups, friends and family members for over thirty years.

Van is a member of Friends of the Boundary Waters and the Superior Hiking Trail Association.

Gerald Strom is a Minnesota native, he attended Hamline University before earning a Ph.D at the University of Illinois in Urbana. He then spent 34 years as a professor of political science at the University of Illinois at Chicago. During his teaching career, he would always find time in the summer to explore and fish in the Boundary Waters Canoe Area and Superior National Forest.

In addition to his professional writing, he has written articles for many different publications, including the *New York Times* and *Boundary Waters Journal*.